Heaven Can Help

The Updated Autobiography

By

Brian Edward Hurst

DEDICATION:

To all my friends and helpers in both worlds I dedicate this book, not forgetting dear Aunt Dorry and Bob & Ann Copley for their continuous support during my early years. I also wish to thank Ramesh Jani for his valuable assistance and practical advice.

OTHER WORKS BY THIS AUTHOR:

Some go Haunting – a reincarnation mystery thriller
The High Hearty Affair – screenplay of Some Go Haunting
Under the Pink Light – a short novel of spiritual awakening
Cinderella's Secret and Other Classical Poems
The Mars Experiment – the story of a future Mars colony

All works are copyright of the author. Links available:
www.brianhurst.com

A MESSAGE TO THE READER:

They always say
In a meaningful way:
"You get punished for doing good!"
I thought: "Oh well,
I'd defy all Hell
To help someone here if I could!"
I little knew
As the long years flew
How many would need my aid.
I did my best
To pass each test,
Had faith in God, and prayed.
For taking birth
On planet Earth
Is a challenge, as all can see.
So many folk
Like zombies spoke:
"There's nought beyond for me!"
But all along
I have proved them wrong,
And the Truth has set them free.
For what can you do
But soldier through
And leave a message of love?
And give the clues
That there's nothing to lose
In trusting Heaven above.
Whatever the race, or whatever the creed,
Let the other folk have their say.
Listen and smile,
And think awhile,
And compromise on the way.
You are your judge and they are theirs,

We all make our Heaven and Hell.
Experience shows
That the bigot knows
Just how to cast his spell
By feeding the flames
With racial names
And epithets as well.
In my own way
I've had my say
And hope that these words ring true,
And that some of the pain
Has not been in vain,
But helped make a good book for you!

Brian Edward Hurst

Above: The author with mother and baby brother Peter, taken at Huntingdon, England in 1940.

Above: My mother, Lillian Daisy Abraham (known as 'Betty') Photo taken prior to her marriage.

1.

Laura, a slim young woman sitting in the rocking chair in my Reseda, California consulting room, looked curiously at me: "I've read so many books on mediumship and so many accounts of other people's experiences that I know there must be *something* in all this business of spirit communication, but I still need to get my own personal evidence to be totally convinced."

"I understand perfectly," I said, "and you're quite right, Laura. What may be excellent proof of communication for one person may not convince another."

She smiled: "You must have a very interesting life, doing what you do. Tell me about it."

"This subject is so vast. Where does one begin? Over the years hundreds of people have told me that I changed their lives for the better, that I gave them a renewed spiritual faith and helped them understand some of the mysteries of life and death. That's an honour and a responsibility that I take seriously, because I care about people."

"Well you certainly have an international reputation," Laura said.

"I've tried to do this work to the best of my ability and sometimes I have failed," I responded, "Many people have been disappointed because they did not make contact with the particular loved one they sought. Instead someone else has often come through and given the most surprising facts and information that the sitter had not expected."

"I call that excellent validation that you really are communicating," Laura said wisely.

"I wish all my clients could see it that way, but some people have a very fixed agenda, and if you don't give them exactly what they want they are dissatisfied."

"I suppose they are emotionally distressed and need to hear something comforting from their loved one."

"Yes, their emotional needs often make them deaf to some very valid information. It is impossible to please all the people all the time!"

"But what a challenge for you!"

"It certainly is," I nodded, "I don't make a lot of money as a medium, but I have been thanked again and again by grateful clients for being affordable. As you can see, if I was in this merely for the money I would charge a great deal more than I do. My main criticism of some of the other mediums is that they are too expensive and most people who are in real need just can't afford them."

"I know. I did my own research," Laura said, "You were the only one I could afford."

"I believe this is spiritual work," I responded, "and when we start charging exorbitant rates, then the credibility of the whole thing comes into question. Of course we have a right to a living and we must pay our bills just as others do, but there should be moderate fees, even though the work is so draining."

"That's what I call integrity," Laura said, "I know that you've given sittings for many years, and you were the discoverer and teacher of James Van Praagh, our most celebrated American medium. Have you written your own book yet?"

"I'm the author of a mystery thriller, entitled *Some Go Haunting*, set in England in 1956. It's a period piece and it's the story of a family dealing with the challenge of a haunted house. The seventeen-year-old protagonist, Richard Buchanan, who is an adopted boy, discovers that he has had a previous life on earth and that he has been brought back to this mysterious house for a purpose. In the course of seeking truth he is also reunited with his biological mother. The story is full of suspense. Strange things happen in the cellar. Two of the characters take part in a successful séance which helps the reader to understand the way in which good mediums work, and the book does have a comforting message and a positive conclusion."

"I'm looking forward to reading it, but you must also write your autobiography, as I'm sure you have some fascinating things to tell us."

I smiled back at her: "My problem is remembering the details. I see so many people in one year, and they take a tape-recording of the whole session away with them. I don't keep any copies. If I did that, the validity of a subsequent sitting with the same person would be undermined. Within a day of the sitting, whatever memory I may have had concerning the evidence I gave the sitter has been erased."

"So it would be quite difficult for you to write about something you can't remember."

"Exactly, as many of the details are private and personal to the people involved. They may not wish their family history or their private pain to be recorded in someone else's book. People are self-conscious about these things. Even if I was able to retain and make notes on what took place during a sitting, a reasonable critic might still say that I was biased or just inventing some of the 'facts' to make myself look good in a book."

"That's true! I hadn't thought of that."

I leaned forward in the canvas director's chair that I use: "Laura, one of my clients, a professor's wife, has recently taken the trouble to make transcripts of the different sittings she had with me. She has kindly given me permission to include some of the material in my book, just as long as I do not use her real name. She says that she came to me as a complete sceptic and was feeling horribly sad about the death of her husband. He meant everything to her and there was unfinished business that troubled her. As a result of the sittings, Mary Hall, as I call her, became a transformed person. She had been so frozen up with grief that she was unable to work. She would sit for long hours in the home, unable to do anything. Normally a sociable person, she was no longer comfortable in the company of other people. Nothing seemed to pull her out of her intense misery and despair. Then a good friend, a well-known television actress, told Mary about her experiences with me. Mary was literally desperate for answers and this motivated her to telephone me for an appointment. I am going to begin my Autobiography with some of the material that Mary, a well-educated lady, spent many hours evaluating. I do not want all her work to be in vain, as she has assured me that I have made a very powerful difference to her whole life. The paralyzing depression has gone, and Mary has now resumed work. She says there was no way I could have known or guessed the information that I gave her, it was so incredible. She tells me I have restored her faith in God and in the reality of an afterlife."

Laura smiled: "It's such an important service you give the community. I just wish that organised religion didn't feel so threatened by this subject."

"Yes," I said, "especially when psychic research reveals that life after death is automatic for everyone on this planet. You don't have to be 'born again' or 'saved'; you don't even have to be Christian to get to heaven. Jesus did say 'In my Father's house are many mansions,' and from our research into this amazing subject it appears that we go into one of many parallel dimensions that are around the earth. We go to people who are very much like ourselves in attitudes, values and belief system. If we're good people we have nothing to fear. We just have to remember that 'Birds of a feather flock together!'"

With those words, and after my usual prayer, I began the sitting with Laura. For the life of me, I cannot remember what eventually came through, but afterwards, when I was still rather 'spaced out', I remember Laura reassuring me that I had done very well and given her accurate information that she had fully understood. The sitting had been a success.

Above: Outside St Mary's Church, Huntingdon in 1954. L to R: Kenneth Hurst, baby Wendy, mother 'Betty,' Joy, Brian and Peter Hurst.

2.

About a year after her first visit to me, Mary Hall, the widow of a college professor, wrote a most helpful and encouraging letter, offering to let me use information and evidence that she had received from her deceased husband through my mediumship. In her neatly typed letter she said: *"I know this is way more than you need, and you probably don't have time to wade through all of it. But I thought I would send it all, so you could have more to choose from when looking for something that might fit in a particular spot. Also I thought you might find it interesting to see how close you come. It is amazing... It is the least that I can do considering what you have done for me. I don't know where I would be today without the belief that you gave me."*

In the excerpts from the sittings, Mary typed my words in a bold font and her responses in a lighter, italicised font, with comments and explanations in between:

Sitting of January 13th, 1997:

He said his knee's all right now. *Oh, is it?* **He had trouble with his knee joint, didn't he? Were they going to do surgery?** *No, it's just that he was in pain all the time. He had been a track star early on and that had ruined his knees.* **The cartilage was gone and it was scraping. He says 'My wife would understand my knee problems. Tell her I have great legs now, and I don't have any knee problems.' They're telling me your husband**

15

was involved with teaching. *Yes, he was.* They keep saying 'apparently a very good educationist.' He was extremely dedicated and I feel this man cared. He was sincere, he was dedicated, and he was hard working. This was a good man, and I think he had helped so many people over the years with his teaching. Did he perhaps connect with scientists and mathematicians? *Yes.* Because I keep seeing mathematical formulae and scientific formulae. I can see algebraic equations. *He was a biological science teacher.* Was this like university college level? *Yes, Community College level.* It was more the teenagers and the young adults I feel that he taught. Does somebody have a dog with an alcoholic name? *An alcoholic name?* A dog with a name like alcohol: bourbon, sherry, brandy, whiskey, something like that? I don't know what it means! Your mother would have known somebody who had an alcoholic dog, or a dog with an alcoholic name. *Oh! My mother's dog Brandy! It was her dog before the last one.* Yes, your husband's seen your mother's alcoholic dog over there. Somebody's told your husband 'Yes, Norman, this is Mary's mother's dog.' *It's strange that that would come through when I'm worried about my dog, and nothing comes through, but Brandy comes through whom I haven't thought about for years.* They deliberately do that sometimes because they want to show that this is not mind reading from

you. You see if I told you everything that was in your mind you might think at the time "Oh that's wonderful! He was brilliant!" But you see, you'd go home and you'd say, "Oh well, I was thinking those things. He was only reading my mind," and there'd be disillusionment settle in later on. But if I tell you things that you're hardly even thinking about, that you aren't even expecting it's going to be much more impressive to you. It's going to make you think and realise that this is not mind reading from you, that I'm really getting it from him.

At a later sitting on April 15th, 1998 there was further talk of dogs, which had an amusing outcome, especially as I had no recollection of the previous sittings. **He's saying something about Freckles or Speckles…It's a name like that. He's seen that animal. I think it's an animal. He says "She never did have a good memory."** *Terrible!* **You were always forgetful, were you?** *He was my memory. I found out later the dog I had in mind, which was his cousin's former dog, was named Pringle, nothing like Freckles or Speckles. I was disappointed. His cousin had already got a new dog whose name I didn't even think to ask.* Turns out it was a Dalmatian named Speckles!

Mary says that her father-in-law has also communicated at nearly every sitting:

There's Norman Hall and George Hall, isn't there? *Yes. That's his father.* **And he's dead too!**

Mary comments: *On one occasion you did a terrific impression of him. It was spooky:*

Who is George Hall? *That's his father.* **He's here with him. He says, "Tell them I'm George Hall!** *That sounds like George!* **A very authoritarian kind of voice.** *Very much so.* **He wanted people to listen to him, you know. He had this kind of quality: the grand old man. Of course he's not really old anymore, but when he comes near to the earth he sometimes comes back into the old personality which seems to be there.** *Well, he wasn't that old when he died, but he was a very kind of...* **forthright! He'd fight for his principles and what he believed in, you know. I think his father was kind of a dominant person.** *Very. Yes.*

Mary commented that her husband's aunt and uncle had been researching the family tree in Scotland, so that many of the ancestral names were now known.

At a sitting on July 23rd, 1997 I apparently said **Are you a canny Capricorn?** *Me?* **Yes. I get the expression "She's a canny Capricorn."** *Canny?* **Canny is, I think, a Scottish word meaning wise and cautious and careful and conservative. You know, not wanting to be outrageous.** *Is that my husband using that term or someone else?* **Somebody else here. Maybe somebody else is**

familiar with astrology. Mary confirmed that her birth sign was Capricorn. **Oh, Norman Hall is here with James Hall. Who are they?** *Norman Hall is my husband.* **Who is James Hall?** *Well, his brother's name is Jim.* **There's a Jim passed over. It's not his brother. Your husband's there with an ancestor who has the name of Jim Hall.**

Mary informed me after the sitting that she had wanted to come on her husband's birthday, but July 23rd was the closest date I could offer. I had no knowledge of this at the time of the sitting. This is what I told her:

Oh, my goodness! You've been putting out something in the home, something on display, something about your husband. *Yes.* **I see a spiritual birthday cake and I can see all these candles on it. And he's not afraid to acknowledge these candles, and he looks young and very handsome.** *Can you see him?* **No, but they're saying to me "Tell Mary her husband is looking very handsome and very good. And he looks much younger." Apparently there's a birthday or something...** *Tomorrow is his birthday. That's why I'm here.* **Oh, I see! He died close to his birthday.** *Yes.* **This was all sort of sudden and shocking. Very dramatic, like a sudden collapse...was this a cerebral accident?** *Stroke.* **I'm touching my head and my neck as I'm speaking to you...I feel like one minute he's here and the next minute he's unconscious, and he's out of his body and he's gone.**

Mary confirms it was a sudden collapse. He had a stroke, and a blood vessel in his brain started to bleed. He became unconscious after the first day. Six days later he was declared brain dead. Mary also remembers: *"from the day that I came home from the hospital for several months I smelt something very strongly that was reminiscent of the way my husband smelled in the hospital. I wondered at the time if it was him, but thought I was crazy."*

I referred to this during the sitting.

I think you've felt him in the bedroom at night haven't you? And you've also smelled him in some strange way. *Yes!*

I'm not sure whether it's the cologne he used or the aftershave or just his sense of smell. *It was an odd smell that I kept smelling after he died.* **It would just come and go very strongly.** *Yes, that's right.* **That was the smell of his astral body. They shed these bodies after a few days or sometimes after a few weeks...and they enter the electrical-mental body. But that (previous) body sometimes does have an odour about it.** *It reminded me of the odour in his hospital room.* **That sometimes is deliberate; so that you associate it with him because that would mean he would be standing there beside you.**

In her transcript, Mary says that the Christmas holidays of 1997 were particularly grim for her. She had booked another sitting for January 13th, 1998. She continues: *"About two days before my appointment with you I got up in the morning and went into the bathroom feeling very desolate. I knew I had to pull myself together. I looked in the mirror and decided my bangs needed trimming. I started to get the scissors and then remembered my husband got on my case once about trimming my bangs and letting the hairs fall in the sink, then cleaning it up. He said it made more sense to put the wastebasket on the sink and let the hairs fall in as you cut them, which is what he did when he or I trimmed his moustache. Remembering this made me laugh and I thought to myself 'Ok, Norm, if this is for real, if you are really there mention this when I see Brian.' By the time I came to see you I had forgotten about this. It was almost the first thing you said. I was flabbergasted. I didn't tell you this at the time"*

Was there a big thing about your husband with a moustache? *He had a moustache.* **Trimming it?** *Yes.* **And something about 'Don't leave the trimmings on the wash basin.'** (Shocked laugh) *Yes.* **Does that make sense? Did you used to go after him and say 'Now look, honey, you've left your trimmings of your moustache all in the washbasin.'?** *He used to get after me for it, and just the other day I was trimming my hair and I was thinking about how he used to do that...setting the waste basket up to catch it.* **I see, because there's definitely...a memory coming here. Someone seems to be amused by this. So it relates to you.** *I was remembering it the other day and thinking, laughing about it myself.* **Oh well,**

that's a funny memory that he seems to share with you…By the way your husband is saying something about he's been with you on your birthday. Has it passed? *Yes.* **He was with you on your birthday…Is that after Christmas or something?** *Yes, it's the 26th.* **He also refers to something about August.** *That's the month he passed away.* **August he passed away, and he also says something about July.** *July is his birthday.* **Really? So one was his birth and one was his death…Of course he's not really dead, as we know, but it looks like he's…um…I felt cold breezes pass my hands just then and it feels chilly. In fact I've got this icy cold sensation all down my back and shoulders like somebody is standing here trying to touch me or trying to give me a kind of pat on the back, saying "Ok, I'm here! I'm here!" And it looks like he's trying to reassure me that he's in command, he's in charge, he's very fine.**

At a further sitting on July 23rd, 1998, Mary was pleased with the following evidential message:

I keep seeing images of little birds, like rare birds…the Spotted Warbler, or something, something that's kind of an endangered species. I think he was interested in these endangered and rare birds, and the birdcalls…Wouldn't he go into the woods and listen and say "I think that's a Spotted Flycatcher or that's a Cuckoo" or something else? *Exactly.* **And he'd talk about**

22

these things to you...Did you pick raspberries then? *Thimbleberries.* You picked some berries in the woods. He remembers that. *Yes, that was in Oregon...*I feel like I'm outside Eugene, am I? *Yes...*Was there a curiosity about owls and bats? *Yes, very much so.* He seems to have been very interested in nocturnal birds...Have you had little ceramic owls in the house? *Well, he did...One of the first things when we started dating, he did an ink drawing of an owl for me.* The owl is significant to you, I know...*And I painted an owl for him for his birthday.* Well, there we are, there's the reference to the owls. This is something so outrageously original that no one else would think of that...The kestrel, the kestrel and the hawk. *Yes.* What does it mean? *He has a kestrel. I have it now.* Is it a living bird? *Yes...*He's not sure; he thinks the bird might see him sometimes. *She acts like it. I've wondered.* Sometimes he said when he's been right close in his spiritual form, in his electrical form, he's reached out and he said she's reacted. He put his hand through the cage. It's a big cage? *Yes...*The bird seems to be sensitive to his energy...he's not sure if the bird sees him, but the bird reacts to him when he goes near. I had no idea you had a kestrel. It's a very unusual pet, and not everybody has a kestrel. And I mean that's something very unusual. *Very.*

Mary comments that the following extract from the sitting of January 13th, 1998, was very clearly the personality of her husband manifesting strongly with his concern about the future of our planet.

Norman is expressing very much concern, not only about the Amazon, but also about the fires in Indonesia and Jakarta and around there, all the burning of the tropical forest. He says that the experts over there believe that this is one of the early stages...the beginning of a very serious destruction of our planet, by destroying the source of oxygen. These trees give off vast amounts of oxygen. We all need it to breathe, and here they are burning all the sources. These people are crazy! They're maniacs! Somebody on earth has got to say 'enough is enough – Stop this burning!' Because reducing all these wonderful green trees and wonderful plants to ashes and things, and wasting all these amazing natural resources to him is the most wicked thing, the wicked rape of the earth. It gets him very upset. And of course now that all the smoke is drifting to Singapore and the east, and they're all having pollution problems and horrible smog problems...he says it's the beginning of a terrible thing, unless people put their foot down and say 'This must stop!' And he wants more of an effort to be made by people here to lobby, lobby, lobby, to stop these crazy people from burning the forests and the jungle, because the jungles are necessary. *Yes.* **Of**

course it will affect the whole climate of the earth if we lose this greenery. It seems to me like he's really got on the bandwagon here. I feel this man's fervour! I feel his enthusiasm! I feel his warning to us that there must be something done about it. Do you know people that are involved with this, trying to fight this? *Yes. Well, my husband was in biology, so he's very much…both of us are environmentalists, you know.* And rightly so. I would agree with you…What can you do? *It's like beating against a brick wall.* Yes. I totally agree with you, Norman. I can't see you, but I can see the wisdom and the soundness of what you're getting upset about, and I wish there was something more I could do personally, but I don't know what we can do. Mary says the same. She feels helpless. Thank you for expressing your feelings. I mean you have a right to feel that way. He says one ecosystem is dependent upon another. They're all interdependent, and he says if you upset the balance in one place, it causes all kinds of diabolical problems somewhere else. *That's right! This is what he taught. He taught environmental biology.* Oh, I see! Then what I'm saying makes total sense, doesn't it? *Oh yes!* It's characteristic of his mind. I know I'm in touch with his mind. I know I'm in touch with his thinking, with his feeling about things. This was his big concern. He doesn't want to just come through and say to you 'Darling, I'm happy,' he wants to come through and give you his love of course, but he wants to say something – that he has a message, that this is sheer, sheer insanity. *It is! Does he have any ideas what we could do?* Oh boy! He's going to work with a team of people over there to impress people in politics, and even in the countries themselves, to cause them to put some restraint or controls over these stupid farmers who are burning just to have the land, so they can grow crops that are not even suited for the type of soil or the type of situation. It's a complete waste because it doesn't work. The soil won't sustain the crops. It certainly won't. They could do things between trees...like (create) long furrows...but have the trees there and have little areas where they grew things. That might work, but they have to compromise with the jungle. They have to compromise with nature and not try to totally destroy, because that's wrong. *Yes.* (To Norman) Thank you, thank you, because Mary understands it very well and apparently that's what you taught, so that's very good proof of your personality coming through. *Yes, it is.*

Looking at Mary's excellent transcript of her sittings, I feel that this can only be the spirit of her deceased husband, Norman Hall communicating from another dimension. To those ignorant critics who maintain that nothing worthwhile is ever received from the spirit world, I would reply "Get your heads out of the sand or you'll never see any daylight." All control freaks have trouble with this subject, **because they are no longer in control!** I understand that knowledge which comes to the person who is unable to receive it is of but little value, but at least the enquirers should have an open mind. They might be surprised at how much more they can understand with an adjustment of their attitude. It would seem that belief in the survival of the human spirit and its ability to communicate with our world represents a big step forward in the evolution of human consciousness. Many are not yet ready to take that step because of fear.

3.

Now that I have presented my reader with some kind of evidence of what may be available during a sitting with a medium, I will deal with some of the events that stand out in my memory. So many people have said to me "We want to know something about *you,* not the people you sat for," that I feel I have to address that legitimate interest. An autobiography is, after all, about the person who writes it. By the nature of things it has to be selective. Much of life is mundane and boring and there are aspects of one's life that are private and personal. This story relates chiefly to the incidents, which I feel, may have led to my becoming what I did, a reliable and honest medium who occasionally failed, but who achieved a sufficient degree of success to impress many thousands of people that this was not clever guesswork or fraud.

How did it all begin? I was born on the cold, snowy evening of March 5th, 1938, in the front bedroom of a tiny terraced cottage at 9, St. Germain Street, Huntingdon, England. A Scottish doctor and a midwife were in attendance, and after a normal labour I emerged weighing eight pounds. (Sadly, all traces of St. Germain Street have now disappeared as the town has developed.)

My father, Kenneth Hurst, aged 23, was a clerk to a Land Agent and had secret dreams of becoming an auctioneer. He was a scrupulously honest, caring and intelligent man of medium height, with green eyes and sleek brown hair parted in the middle, in the fashion of his day. Somewhat jumpy and nervous, he had the habit of dancing from one foot to the other when he became agitated or impatient. Because of a tendency to asthmatic attacks he would speak quickly, taking audible breaths in the middle of a longer sentence. Throughout his whole life he had a gentlemanly quality, never used bad language, and was extremely studious, being interested in Esperanto and Pitman's shorthand, which he learned to write rapidly. He was fond of light opera, and although not gifted with a great singing voice, he would entertain family and friends with hammed-up numbers from musical shows that caught his fancy at the time. For several years he owned a ventriloquist's doll that he named 'Charlie' and he would willingly entertain the neighbourhood children at birthday parties. Like most Geminis he had a good sense of humour and a ready wit. Having a Leo Moon he also liked performing.

My mother, Lillian Daisy (nee Abraham), hated both her Christian names, and was from her late teens known as 'Betty.' She had left school at fourteen and was later employed as a waitress at Shepherd's Café in Huntingdon High Street. She had chestnut brown hair, a beautiful peaches-and-cream complexion and alert, brown, mischievous eyes. She met my father at the Papworth Everard Flower Show and dance at the end of nineteen thirty-five. Apparently he tried to rush her into marriage after only three weeks, so from his side it appears to have been love at first sight. My mother, a somewhat more cautious Capricorn, took a little longer to make up her mind. They were finally married on January 30th, nineteen thirty-seven at St. Mary's Church, Huntingdon. As a wedding present, my mother's boss, Mr. Frederick Shepherd a well-known caterer of Huntingdon, gave the happy couple a large cake.

My parents began their married life in a romantic thatched cottage in the village of Kings Ripton. The cottage was owned at the time by my grandmother who allowed her daughter to rent it for five shillings a week. It had no flush toilet and no electricity and a paraffin lamp was burned on the table each night. Later, when my mother became pregnant, she missed the somewhat better facilities that Huntingdon had to offer. A grey-bricked terraced cottage had become vacant in St. Germain Street and my parents then moved back to the town, awaiting my birth on March 5th.

One night to my mother's horror, she discovered a bed bug crawling across my blanket. Upon examination of the old, brown wallpaper, my parents found that the whole place was badly infested with bugs and would need urgent fumigation. Concerned for the health risks to a small baby, my father desperately looked around for alternative accommodation. Luckily, the senior mistress of Huntingdon Grammar School, Miss McClelland, needed a cook and housekeeper. My mother was interviewed and got the job, enabling the three of us to move into rooms in a big house in the nearby village of Godmanchester, which lay across the other side of the River Ouse. This turned out to be only a temporary solution to our housing problem as my mother again became pregnant, suffering so acutely from morning sickness that it was obvious the housekeeping position could not last. The Scottish physician, Dr. Connan who had delivered me, used his influence to get us a small council house at 36 Priory Road, Huntingdon at a reasonable rent.

The new house had a small front garden with fragrant syringa growing near the gate, a brown, wooden fence that enabled me to peep through at passing dogs and people, and a good-sized back garden where I delighted in digging a few holes. My mother obtained some rabbit hutches and soon filled them with munching bunnies. I was solemnly cautioned not to put my small fingers anywhere near the wire as the occupants might bite. The long back garden was soon growing rows of cabbages, beans and potatoes planted by my mother's father, Edward Abraham. He was the chief gardener as my father was never much interested in those days.

Apparently I was such a cute baby, that all the local teenage girls wanted to take me out for a walk in my pram. My mother eventually allowed a girl named Barbara to do this, until a horror story got back from a concerned neighbour. This particular neighbour had been sitting on a seat at the bottom of a hill in a small local park known as 'Castle Hills.' Looking up, she saw Barbara pushing my pram towards a steep path that descended between clumps of stinging nettles. The girl suddenly let go of the pram and I was propelled sharply down in the neighbour's direction. Unfortunately a molehill diverted the pram, tipped it over and I was thrown into the thick grass near the nettles. Hearing my loud screams, the neighbour intervened, picked me up and ordered Barbara to take me home immediately. I was unhurt but extremely frightened. Needless to say, my mother never allowed anyone else to take me out after she heard of that incident.

I sometimes wonder whether that traumatic experience of unexpectedly flying through the air made me fearful, in later years, of the school gymnasium where I was never able to do handstands on the box or climb very high on the beams for fear of falling. As a teenager I positively dreaded the gym period and was totally unable to accomplish anything too advanced to the extreme annoyance of the teacher who believed that I was merely disobedient. Today I still find it difficult to ride on overhead cable cars and I stay far away from roller coasters and anything else that drops suddenly. Such is the power of early conditioning.

September 1939 saw the outbreak of the Second World War. My young father was called up for military service, and as luck would have it, was suffering from acute tonsillitis and what was to be the beginning of a bout of very bad health. He arrived in Aldershot, Hampshire, on 14th September. His unit had already moved to Ash Vale ready for embarkation to France, but as he had developed asthma in addition to the tonsillitis he was rapidly admitted to the military hospital. This illness probably saved his life, as many of those who left for

France never returned, and in my father's case being sick turned out to be a very good thing!

After his recovery, Dad became a Regimental Accountant attached to the Royal Army Ordnance Corps in Aldershot. He was with them until nineteen forty-three when he answered an advertisement for a Staff Secretary at The War Office in London. There he became Personal Assistant to Brigadier Storar, then Brigadier Connan (brother to my mother's physician) and later, Brigadier Butler. The relationship with all three men was excellent, and regular communications were received from them long after the war was ended. My father advanced in rank from Lance Corporal to Corporal; then Lance Sergeant to Sergeant, and eventually Staff Quartermaster Sergeant. He was assigned to a new branch which opened at The War Office dealing with Planning, Progress and Production in The Royal Electrical Mechanical Engineers (R.E.M.E) and there he worked as personal assistant to the Deputy Director of Mechanical Engineers. My father remained with The War Office until general demobilisation in nineteen forty-eight. During much of that time he lodged with a Mrs. Ridout who kept a boarding house for military personnel in south London and Dad was only able to get home at occasional weekends when he had the money.

My brother Peter was born in January nineteen forty. He was so sick and frail that he almost died. During my mother's confinement my loving grandmother Emma Abraham took care of me. I would be given dominoes or playing cards to keep me amused, and my favourite occupation was to sit out in the back yard and constantly pour water from one bottle to another. My grandfather showed me how to make music by hitting the different bottles with an old spoon. Later, my grandmother had some chickens that I had to beware of. The young roosters would strut about and sometimes fly up in my face. One of them became an aggressive little devil and ultimately had to be despatched for Christmas dinner.

My grandfather Edward was an ardent fisherman and kept a small punt chained to a willow tree down at the nearby River Ouse. We had many happy picnics by the river in summertime. Grandfather knew where to pick the best mushrooms and blackberries when in season. He would occasionally shoot a rabbit and bring it back for granny to skin and cook. I hated the smell and taste of rabbit meat, and as I had pet rabbits at home I think that added to my natural aversion to eating them.

Meanwhile, *The Daily Mirror* newspaper would drop through the letterbox of the Priory Road council house, and I would see large, black cartoons of a frightening monster called Hitler. My mother often seemed moody and irritable and I was made to eat every portion of food put in front of me, being constantly told that children were starving in India and that I was lucky to have anything to eat at all! Baby Peter was quite difficult to feed as he would fuss constantly and have loud temper tantrums if he didn't get everything he wanted. With no father present to discipline us my mother had to play the challenging role of both parents. It must have been tremendously difficult for her.

After my brother's birth, there was definite sibling rivalry, especially when my mother told me that my baby brother needed *all* her attention and I was now big enough to help her with the household chores.

I remember looking forward to my father's homecomings because he was cheerful and always made a fuss of me. He brought me coloured pencils, drawing books and obsolete maps that had been discarded from The War Office. The back of each map made an excellent drawing surface. I would stand at the front gate waiting for Dad to come up the road with his bouncy walk wearing his khaki uniform, and carrying his kit bag that always contained a few surprises. Later, in the small scullery I would climb on his lap and stare into his humorous green eyes, begging him to play 'gee gees' with me. Seated on his knee I would be transformed into a jockey jumping Beecher's Brook and racing round Tottenham Corner to the winning post. He bought me a small engine on wheels and I would delight in sitting astride this toy and making loud noises as I pushed myself up and down the garden path. My father seemed to have endless patience, in contrast to my exasperated mother who would scream and shout daily at her hyperactive little bundle of mischief.

I loved listening to the 'wireless', especially to the daily adventures of detective 'Dick Barton – Special

Agent' which came on for fifteen minutes at 6.45p.m. Monday to Friday. There would also be good comedy programmes at lunchtime, such as 'Workers' Playtime' in which the laughter of the audience was so outrageous and spontaneous that it added tremendously to the fun! I remember Elsie and Doris Waters and some of the rude jokes that they would tell, much to my father's disapproval. He was rather old-fashioned about such things and occasionally I would be ushered out of the room or the wireless turned off.

Using the discarded maps my father brought home I began to take an interest in copying some of the strip cartoons from *The Daily Mirror.* One cartoon was about a strong man named 'Garth,' and in one of the stories a character named Professor Lumiere hypnotised Garth and took him back into the memory of a previous life on earth. Garth had been programmed to utter the word 'karma' in the event of an emergency, and that was where I first saw that word now used in so much metaphysical literature. The strip was read by thousands of other children, but to me it had a peculiar fascination. Little did I realise that many years later I would be lecturing on those topics and demonstrating unusual powers of mind.

I think my first conscious encounter with death, and what it entails, came when my mother and I were going shopping, and happened to be passing through St. Germain Street where I was born. We had passed the old Huntingdon Brewery with its characteristic smell of hops, its clinking of bottles and its puffing of steam, when I decided to run ahead to the end terraced cottage that was the home of my great-grandma, Mary Read (nee Mallet). Granny Read was a buxom, grey-haired lady who in her earlier days had won beauty competitions. Her husband, David Read, had worked for the Huntingdon Breweries for many years before passing away. My great-grandma always made a fuss of me when we stopped by to see her. The door of the house was ajar, so I pushed it open and went inside. Instead of Granny Read greeting me there was a total stranger.

"What do you want, little boy?" this tall lady asked me in a rather loud, shrill voice.

"I want my grandma," I said, staring up with a puzzled expression.

"Your grandma doesn't live here anymore," the lady replied, "Have you got the right house?"

I remember thinking: "I know this is the right house and my grandma should be here."

Just then my mother arrived on the scene and apologised to the strange lady.

"Your grandma's gone to be with the angels up in Heaven," I was told.

It was quite a shock to me, as that was the first time my mother had mentioned it. We had always called on Granny Read, and now she had gone away forever. I was very upset to hear it. Later, when we had thunderstorms, my mother told me not to be frightened as it was only the coal being delivered to the angels, and that was why there was such a loud noise from the sky. I was later told that my classic reply was: "Mummy the angels have an awful lot of coal, don't they?"

I often wondered whether Granny Read was warm enough up there!

Above: My mother holding Granny Read's cat at the front door of the St. Germain Street terraced house in Huntingdon.

4.

My first day at Huntingdon County Primary School was in September 1943. I was left in charge of Miss Mills, a slim young lady with neatly permanent-waved hair and horn-rimmed glasses. She referred to us all as 'the babies' and we were seated at tiny individual desks in single rows. Miss Mills was very patient and never shouted at any child. Her voice was very musical, and she told delightful stories about the letters of the alphabet. I still remember the Dick and Jane books, and having to stare hard at the puzzling rows of black shapes on each page. Because of previous help from my mother and grandmother I quickly learned to read, and to this day I am eternally grateful to the team of dedicated teachers who used phonic methods to help me decode the various letter combinations. When the first letter of the alphabet makes so many different sounds it is not surprising that many children find this confusing and give up. (e.g. "Watch any cat - a cat hates all wet grass.")

Miss Scott was the Headmistress. She was short, extremely plain, with straight grey hair and two teeth that protruded at the front. She had penetrating eyes behind owl-like glasses, and we were always nervous when she entered the classroom to test us. I think she was a kind and dedicated soul whose bark was worse than her bite. She made it clear that she was in charge and no one dared to question that. She used the cane on a number of naughty children and sometimes on those who were persistently late for school.

Sometime during our idyllic first year with the lovely Miss Mills, we were all issued with gas masks, a fact that brought home to us the reality of the current war. We had gas mask drill on a regular basis. I hated the smell of the rubber and the claustrophobic sensation of my face being enclosed. The only fun part was the rude raspberry noise we could produce when exhaling forcefully through the curious nosepiece.

Those war years must have been incredibly difficult for my long-suffering mother. She was quite an emotional person, easily hurt by criticism, and there were many occasions on which I saw her break down and cry. Sometimes in desperation she would turn to us and say "If you don't behave yourselves I'll put my hat and coat on and just leave you to get on with it!" Small children believe these words and feel their impact deeply. My father was absent most of the time and the army pay provided only for the bare necessities. Grandma Abraham helped immensely by buying us clothes and shoes. I was her favourite grandchild and could do no wrong. In some ways, looking back, I think I was much closer to her than I was to my own mother. Later, we learned, our parents had been going through marital stress caused by the forced separation, and that had contributed to my mother's changing moods and sudden outbursts of tears.

Towards the end of the war I remember opening *The Daily Mirror* to a comic strip entitled 'Jane.' She was a glamour girl who often appeared in frilly underwear, and she had a soldier boyfriend named Georgie. To my utter amazement one of the frames had Jane totally nude. I had had no idea prior to that time that pubic hair existed. When I made a comment about this, my mother snatched away the newspaper sharply telling me that 'Jane' wasn't meant for little boys to read. I was puzzled by this outburst and I learned many years later that Jane's nudity coincided with the advance of the Allied Forces to the German front. It was *The Daily Mirror's* way of cheering and encouraging our troops to win.

V.E. day marked the end of the war in Europe. People put out flags in the streets of Huntingdon, and there were noisy celebrations. Every street had a magnificent party. American servicemen from the nearby Base at Alconbury brought candies, cakes and cookies and distributed them to the local people. Priory Road was closed to traffic and had rows of folding tables full of the kind of goodies we had not seen for several years. Everyone seemed light-hearted and friendly.

That May 1945, my mother had other things on her mind. She was big with her third child and was dearly hoping for a little girl. When the birth became imminent, Peter was taken care of by my mother's older sister, Elsie, who now lived in the thatched cottage at Kings Ripton where I was conceived. I was sent to the nearby town of St. Ives to stay with my father's father and his lovely second wife, whom I called 'Auntie Mary.' They had a small bungalow on the corner of London Road outside the town. After my father's mother had died of tuberculosis, my grandfather, Arthur John Hurst had found himself unable to cope. He had hired a slim, cheerful, silver-haired lady named Maud Mary Everett to be his cook and housekeeper. Soon afterwards, they were married.

Auntie Mary and Granddad had a large garden surrounding the bungalow, which was named 'The Orchard.' A portion of the land was wired off for chickens, and there were many fruit and nut trees. In May, everything was in full blossom. Although I missed my mother, and knew the reason for our separation, I was in heaven exploring the expansive garden and collecting the eggs from the hen house. Being quite thin, I was just able to squeeze through the hole in the door used by the chickens. For some reason that was more fun than entering in the conventional manner. I also learned that some of the eggs were fakes. They were supposed to fool the hens to lay more! Auntie Mary showed me how to carefully reach under a broody hen without getting pecked.

A few days later Grandfather announced that my father's brother Noel had been released from a German concentration camp after two years of imprisonment, and that he would be coming to visit us the next day. Auntie Mary gave me coloured pencils and asked me to do a large 'Welcome Home' sign, and when Noel arrived he was greeted with great emotion by all of us.

Eventually my mother gave birth to a baby girl on the evening of May 25th. Joy Mary as she was named, had the unusual combination of blonde hair and brown eyes, and the whole family welcomed her. I returned home and because my mother was busy with constant washing and ironing I spent quite a lot of time with our next door neighbour, Mrs. Ballm. 'Auntie Ballm' as I called her, was certainly one of the sweetest ladies I have ever known and her friendship with our family lasted for many years. She regularly cut out the comic strips from the *Daily Mail*, pinned them together in sequence and let me have them to read. I followed the adventures of 'Teddy Tail' and 'Rupert' with great enthusiasm. I used 'Auntie Ballm' as the model for the character of Aunt Laura in my first novel 'Some go Haunting,' which is the story of a family's encounter with a haunted house in 1956 England.

Some researchers investigating the cause of psychic ability in certain people have asked whether the psychics had ever experienced a strong electric shock during their early years. To address that issue I tell the following anecdote:

Whenever I had visited my Grandma Abraham, she would talk to me seriously about the need for me to help my mother with the housework. Everything at home seemed to get piled up and in a horrible mess. I think my mother was going through a bad time, and this was reflected in her neglect of the home environment.

One Friday my father was due home for his weekend leave from The War Office. My mother had mops and dusters out and I was given the task of applying wax polish to the linoleum strip at the edge of the carpet. As I was kneeling down with the duster I noticed some white fluffy substance blocking a hole in a power point that was placed low on the skirting board. I found a small metal screwdriver that my mother had left beside the wireless, and I proceeded to poke the screwdriver into the hole to get rid of the obstruction. Suddenly I received a violent jolt and was thrown backwards across the carpet wondering what had hit me. Shortly after that experience I remember having strange dreams in which I was floating out of my body and swimming through a rainbow of colours. When I reached the pink level I would feel myself being sucked down and waking up in a panic, my heart racing, as I would fall back into my body. In some of the dreams I would be hanging upside down over a large dark chasm feeling myself swinging backwards and forwards as though suspended from a rope. I would be consumed by a fear of falling. My whole body would tingle with a sensation of pins and needles, as though I was being charged with electricity. I would usually wake up in fear and panic. Sometimes I would hear voices speaking to me in the darkness of the bedroom and see strange faces floating about in the air. These experiences were so frightening that I began to ask my mother for a small night-light. Looking back, I really believe that the strong electric shock I received may well have been responsible for the opening up of my psychic awareness, and whether the experience was genuinely accidental or in some way 'planned', who is to say?

Above: Arthur John Hurst with 2nd wife "Auntie Mary."

Above: Kenneth Hurst in army uniform, taken early 1940's

5.

As 'coming events cast their shadows before', I know now that my family was given certain signs that I was destined to do unusual work in the world. My mother told me of a rather frightening incident that had occurred while I was a young baby and she was alone in the house.

"It was shortly after the war had broken out and your father had gone into the army. I was feeling very worried and upset about our separation. I was lying in bed trying to read a book by the natural light from the upstairs window. The sun had already gone down and the bedroom began to get dark, so I thought it was time to sleep. I put the book on the bedside table and glanced at you lying in your cot at the foot of my bed. You were about eighteen months old, I think. As I looked in your direction I saw this dark, grey misty shape suddenly appear beside your cot. I was so frightened I was paralysed, and my heart was beating very fast. I stared at this strange shape at the foot of the bed and I remember thinking for a moment that someone must have crept into the room while I wasn't looking. I almost expected to be attacked, but then to my amazement the shape raised an arm and pointed at you lying in your cot fast asleep. I was very frightened and wished with all my strength that the thing would disappear. As soon as I thought that, to my great relief, it was suddenly gone. I knew instinctively that the dark shape wasn't something from this world. It had to come from somewhere else. I dived under the bedclothes and I couldn't sleep for a long time. It was very disturbing because it was so *real*. Later, when I told your father about it, he wondered whether it was the spirit of his dead brother Frank who had died in the motor cycle accident at the age of twenty."

My mother also recollected another strange incident when my brother and I were visiting my grandmother. Mum was alone in the house when she heard a knock at the door. Upon opening it, she was greeted by a cheerful gypsy selling lavender, lace and clothes pegs. My mother bought some pegs and other items and the delighted gypsy began fortune telling.

"You've got a lucky face, my dear! Your husband won't die in the war. You've got two boys at the moment. The youngest one will give you problems, the oldest one will travel far and be very famous, you mark my words! You'll have a little girl later on and I see the loss of a child. You'll get over it. It's a baby that doesn't really want to come here."

These remarkable predictions turned out to be perfectly true. Many years later I learned that my mother had had a miscarriage two years before my sister Joy was born. My brother did have many health problems as he grew up, and I certainly travelled far and became well known in the metaphysical community.

In spite of post-war shortages and rationing, the early days at Priory Road seemed idyllic. Then one day while visiting my grandma Abraham at Newtown, a suburb of Huntingdon, I noticed my grandfather Edward sitting on a chair with his right trousers leg rolled up, staring mournfully at an angry red lump beneath his knee.

"It's not getting any better," he said.

Granny bent down to examine the area that was oozing with pus.

"What have you done to it? There are maggots crawling out of it!"

I went over to look, and indeed there were little white maggots emerging. I found this very shocking. Shortly afterwards, grandfather was diagnosed with cancer of the bone. Within a few months he was in such severe pain that amputation of the lower leg became necessary. During his illness he showed much bravery and even insisted upon helping my mother with the gardening, planting of vegetables and harvesting of potatoes, something my father could not do because he was still working in London.

I noticed that grandfather was smoking almost constantly and had yellow-stained fingers. Several times he told me never to take up the habit when I grew up and I have followed his advice. After the amputation of his right leg above the knee he moved around for a short time on crutches. Once while visiting us and initially frightening me by the absence of his leg, I noticed him trying to reach cigarette ends thrown on the path outside our gate.

"Pick those up for me, Bri, will you?"

"Why, Granddad?"

"I don't have money for cigarettes, but I can roll those dog ends into new ones and smoke them."

I remember feeling terribly sorry for him. As his illness progressed and he was confined to a bed in a downstairs sitting room, I would often take him a pocketful of cigarette ends I had picked up outside one of the pubs in town. I found that the pubs frequented by American servicemen were the best bet for longer dog ends. As a child of nine, this did not seem such a degrading thing to do. After all, the cigarettes gave granddad pleasure in his final illness. My grandmother gave me a cigarette-rolling machine and some packets of rice paper, and I would spend many an hour beside my dying grandfather pulling the tobacco from the dog ends, stuffing it between the rollers and turning out brand new 'ciggies' for him to smoke.

By December 1947, granddad was being heavily sedated. He would sing Christian hymns during his lucid moments, and once when I looked in upon him, he stared straight past me and said with unbelievable terror:

"Don't let that old man standing over there get me, will you?"

Surprised, I turned around, but was unable to see anything.

Granddad died on December 23rd, and was cremated, his ashes being placed in the cemetery plot where his eldest son 'Ted' had been buried. Some years earlier, 'Uncle Ted' (William George Edward) had haemorrhaged after a tonsillectomy at the local hospital, and to the rage and disgust of my grandmother, had died from alleged negligence by the night nursing staff. The day after granddad's funeral I was taken to see the flowers at the burial plot, and I thought what a sad Christmas it had been for my red-eyed grandmother.

Within a week of my visit to the cemetery, I began having nightmares. I saw my grandfather with his crutches rising up from a pool of red water. Then the crutches disappeared and he stood there staring at me, like a wooden soldier with one leg. He would talk to me, but the voice sounded as though it was at the end of a long tunnel, and had a muffled quality that made it almost impossible for me to distinguish the words. He appeared to be asking for prayers. Soon the pool of blood-like water would lap around my feet and I would try to run as I saw my grandfather melting away into a kind of mist. Looking back on these dreams now, with some insight, I realise that my grandfather had been in active service during the First World War and had probably killed some men in combat. Perhaps the blood around him symbolised his sense of guilt over the blood he had been forced to shed at that time. He was probably passing through the immediate after-death stage of his own life evaluation where he saw troubling events from his past dramatized as scenes around him. Psychic research reveals that immediately after death all people pass through this 'life review' where they are called upon to 'judge' or evaluate the earthly experiences they have left behind. From my memories of these nightmares it would seem that I was probably sharing some of granddad's life review. Hopefully the presence of his bewildered little grandson in this collective experience was able to alleviate some of the darkness of its content.

Every night, when the lights were turned out, I would see grandfather standing there, looking at me with his pale blue eyes. Sometimes he would try to touch me and I would dive under the bedclothes. I knew that he should be in Heaven and I could never understand at that time why he kept coming to visit me. I believe these manifestations were an early sign of my mediumship.

I told my mother about the frightening experiences and admitted that I was scared of the dark. She was very sympathetic and allowed me to have a night-light burning. I also had a small flashlight under my pillow in case the candle went out. Almost immediately the visitations of my grandfather ended. I know that my mother talked with my grandma about this, and my grandma would cuddle me and kiss me and tell me I was going to be all right.

My father finished his military career in 1948 and returned to us at Priory Road. Although jobs were difficult to find, dad's excellent references and his skill at Pitman's shorthand and accounting landed him a job in the Huntingdon County Surveyor's office, where he worked under the supervision of Mr. Thomas Longstaff, the County Architect.

As my young sister was getting older, she needed her own bedroom and the house at Priory Road became too small. We were allowed to move to a larger council house in Cowper Road and soon I began taking piano lessons with one of our middle-aged neighbours, Mr. Harold Dew. The cost was one shilling and threepence for half an hour. My ambitious grandmother had visions of me becoming a concert pianist. The sad reality was that this small boy would much rather have stayed at home and listened to the radio plays on 'Children's Hour'. Mr. Dew conducted the piano lessons in his small front sitting room. He would often be eating kippers and the place would smell accordingly. Mrs. Dew was a quiet little lady whom I seldom saw. If I arrived a few minutes early I would listen to the tail end of the previous pupil's lesson. She was a tall girl named Jillian Skerry, who played with great skill, and Mr. Dew would turn and say, "That's how *you* will play if you only do your practice." Jillian later became a well-known musician in the local town community.

The move to Cowper Road seemed to coincide with a period of personal bad health. Looking back, I am sure that our limited diet of white bread, potatoes, mincemeat and steamed cabbage was quite inadequate for a growing child. I was afflicted with a number of painful boils on my low back and bottom area. My mother would apply a hot kaolin poultice, which would nearly make me jump through the ceiling, and after several unpleasant episodes of tears and screaming it was discovered that the application of common Vaseline to the skin prior to the poultice would immediately prevent the horrible burning sensation.

I had not long recovered from a bad carbuncle on my bottom when the area below my right knee began to swell and give much pain. My mother thought that a spider had bitten me, which was highly possible because of the large number of them in the garden. The bite soon turned septic and I was confined to bed, while an angry redness moved steadily up my thigh. I thought about my deceased grandfather and how he must have suffered. I was unable to walk because of the sensitivity of the knee, and I was also frightened that I might need a similar amputation. Such are the scenarios that run through a child's mind. Dr. Forbes came to visit me, diagnosed septicaemia, and my bottom was pumped full of penicillin. It saved my life.

I moved into the final class at Huntingdon County Primary School and was taught by Mr. Frank Holmes, a tall grey-haired man who tried to explain to us the mysteries of decimals and fractions. I was never much good at mathematics, I'm afraid, but my love of drawing and cartooning and daydreaming showed that I had a powerful inner life that others were not always sensitive to. I hated going out on to the football field and often deliberately forgot my football boots or my shorts so that I was left behind in the classroom to do more of my beloved drawings. Consequently I had few friends and was something of a loner. Because I was a sensitive boy with a ready smile and a desire to please, I got picked on by some of the town's ruffians. In fact there were several mean little bullies, who had probably been abused by their own poverty-stricken parents, and who were only too eager to transfer their rage upon me because I was not by nature aggressive. In fact I was rather a timid boy who was seen as something of a sissy because I was no good at sports and I sometimes played with the girls in the street. One of those girls, whom I still remember with affection, taught me some of the facts of life while we were lying in a hayfield. We experimented in childlike ways a number of times whenever we were in the fields together until one day she refused to do it, saying that she didn't want to have a baby. Obviously her mother had warned her of the consequences of such actions and she had not realised that a boy of ten could hardly be a threat. She was a little older so was probably aware of changes in her body and the need for assuming an attitude of modesty. As far as I am concerned that childhood experimentation was just one of those things. It neither helped nor harmed me. I still remember those early romps in the hayfield with positive emotion, because nothing further happened with a member of the opposite sex until I was in my late teens. Ah! Such is childhood!

In the meantime, Mr. Frank Holmes was an excellent teacher, and he prepared us to take the scholarship examination, which would determine whether we continued our education at the Huntingdon Grammar School or the Secondary Modern. At weekends I would travel on the bus to Mr. Holmes' residence in Hemingford Grey for extra coaching in Arithmetic, which was my weak subject. My parents gave me every encouragement to pass the exam and I fulfilled their expectations. Grandma Abraham, and my mother's sister Joan, with typical generosity, bought my green blazer and short grey pants for the new school I was to attend. Yet I still remember looking at the new clothes up in my bedroom and feeling unbelievably sad and afraid of the changes I was about to make.

This beautiful school was demolished and moved across the road to a new complex adjoining Hinchingbrooke Castle on Brampton Road, Huntingdon.

6.

Friends of my father would sometimes joke that if he opened his wallet the moths would fly out! My mother complained all the time about his reluctance to give her any spare money for clothes. My father was equally parsimonious regarding his own wardrobe and hung on to one "teddy bear" coat for over thirty years. In all fairness it could not have been easy on his salary to keep growing boys in clothes and shoes in post-war Britain. Grandma Abraham was the good angel who came to our rescue on so many occasions. I think I was not allowed to join the Boy Scouts because it would have incurred extra expense for uniform and various camping trips. Grandma Abraham realised that I ought to belong to something in the town that would keep me out of mischief during the weekends.

St. Mary's Church happened to want a few more choirboys, and as the uniform was absolutely free, I was sent along to speak to the vicar, a tall, slightly bald, red-faced Scotsman named Reverend Morris. I discovered that my grandma had already had a long talk with him, and as a result I was accepted into the choir for Matins at eleven a.m. and Evensong at six-thirty p.m. A number of grownups also sang in the choir, and my knees were knocking as I walked, angelically attired, with the other boys into the choir stalls for the service to begin. Mr. Graves, the organist, played some impressive sounding notes and the music resounded from the huge pipes behind me, sending electric tingles up and down my spine.

Sometime later, during the sermon which seemed endless and totally above my comprehension, there was a tinny rattling from the opposite choir stall. A lady with sharp brown eyes and a long chin resembling a shoe toe began fumbling on the seat beside her for a throat pastille. She appeared to have been successful as she glanced furtively around before speedily popping something into her mouth. I then watched with utter fascination as this chin moved up and down for the next five minutes. I had just seen "The Wizard of Oz" at the local *Grand Cinema,* and had a sudden disconcerting image of this respectable lady taking off on a broomstick and cackling down at the church congregation.

Having been inveigled into the choir, something I didn't particularly enjoy, I was also urged to attend Sunday school in the afternoon. Lunch was hurriedly squeezed somewhere between the two events. I had an old decrepit bicycle that clicked and clanked, and I remember that it was of enormous value at that time, though somewhat demanding of oil to silence the squeaks.

My mother had a younger brother christened Ernest. He had married an Austrian woman named Maria at the outbreak of the war, so that she would not be interned as an alien and a possible threat to security. I think my uncle had loved her, but she later had an affair with another man, which led to the break-up of the marriage. Disillusioned, my uncle went back to live with his mother at her new residence in the High Street. As a boy, Ernest had been dark-skinned and wavy-haired, and once, with the help of a little makeup and costume he had entered a fancy dress as a black minstrel. As a result of this event he acquired the embarrassing nickname of 'Nigger.' Even his mother called him this, and his young nephews knew him as 'Uncle Nigger.' (I apologise to my esteemed African readers for the use of this now undesirable word, but at that time it was used as a term of affection only) Uncle Nigger was tall and heavily built with a deep voice and a rather earnest expression on his face (pardon the pun). He drove a van for a radio and television servicing company known as Belcher's Radio. That caused a few giggles in the family. Through him, however, I was able to experience television for the first time at my grandmother's house. Admittedly the screen was small and the box quite large by today's standards, but I enjoyed watching Annette Mills, sister of the famous movie star John Mills, as she played a grand piano, while Muffin the Mule, a delightful animal puppet would dance from strings on the shiny piano top. Annette Mills was later killed in a tragic car accident that shocked the country.

There was an old stable in the back yard of the High Street house, and Uncle Nigger had this as his rather messy workshop. It was full of all kinds of electrical gadgets he had salvaged, auto-change record players that he was fixing, broken movie projectors and old radios. Later, my uncle worked as a projectionist at the local Hippodrome Cinema in Huntingdon High Street, and I had the frequent opportunity to go up in the projection room, see the huge reels of film whirring through the machines and collect clippings from some of the MGM Technicolor movies. I wish I still had that wonderful box of clippings and the viewer that went with them.

One day Uncle Nigger told my mother and me about an intriguing David Niven movie that was showing. It must have impressed him deeply because he urged us both to see it.

"It's called *'A Matter of Life and Death'*," he said, "And it's about a pilot who should have died in a plane crash. He falls in the ocean and survives. Then he's rescued but needs to have brain surgery. While he's on the operating table this French spirit comes to take the pilot's spirit up the Stairway to Heaven. The film then goes into black and white while the pilot's pleading his case before a judge in Heaven. It's quite funny to see the men who died in the war lining up to get their wings wrapped in cellophane."

The film sounded so unusual that we took my uncle's advice and saw it the very next evening. I still remember fantasising about how good it might be to have a French guide from Heaven who could offer protection and support to me while I was still alive on the earth. Little did I know that many years later I was to have my wish fulfilled in an extraordinary way.

The school summer holidays of 1949 passed all too quickly. I had said goodbye to Mr. Holmes and Huntingdon County Primary, and as I had passed the scholarship, the eleven-plus as it was called, to enter the local Grammar School, I became the proud possessor of a new bicycle as a reward. My old machine was passed on to my brother.

Early in September, with butterflies in my stomach, I cycled to the new school building, which lay nestled in green playing fields below the level of the Brampton Road on the south side of the town. To the west of that road we had a real castle, which had been the family residence of Lord Hinchingbrooke, and where it was rumoured there were ghosts, secret passages and things that went bump in the night. Brampton Road was lined with horse chestnut trees, which to every schoolboy's delight yielded large numbers of brown 'conkers'. Soon these would be threaded on strings, and the hardest 'conker', which resisted the impact of all others, would be traded for comic books or sweets. However, on that morning 'conkers' was the farthest thing from my mind.

Chaining my new bicycle nervously to a metal rack by the side of the school, I was ushered by prefects wearing red and green ringed caps into the large assembly hall. There I was seated with other nervous boys on the front row, looking up at a stage filled with the oddest assortment of people I had ever seen. I recognised Miss Williams, the French teacher, from the bright red costume she usually wore. She had once been our Sunday school teacher at St. Mary's. Her brown eyes beamed down at us from behind rimless glasses, and she seemed the most benevolent person there, because I knew her. Several of the elderly male teachers had a distinctly grim appearance, no doubt anticipating their forthcoming encounters with a new set of little horrors!

The Headmaster, Mr. Rowntree, who had distant relatives involved in the cocoa and chocolate business, entered wearing a long, black gown that flowed out behind him. He was tall and slender and with his glasses looked somewhat like the actor Will Hay. He cleared his throat twice (a characteristic habit) and morning prayers began.

Afterwards our names were called and we were told to accompany respective form teachers to our new classrooms. A middle-aged lady wearing a short green gymslip and slightly wrinkled wool stockings led us across a quadrangle, through swing doors, up some stairs and along a corridor to room number two. There we were seated behind ink-stained and graffiti-carved desks as we listened to this kindly soul, her head tilted to one side as she explained to us the various school rules. Her name was Miss Pearson, and she told us that we were very privileged to have the opportunity to receive an education that many others could not enjoy. We were given our timetable for the week and a plan of the school was put on the blackboard.

There were many changes of rooms, and I recall having moments of sheer panic when my timetable mysteriously disappeared from my school satchel and I couldn't remember my destination.

The biggest nightmare of my first day at the new school was to occur after I had eaten lunch with everyone else in the assembly hall. Curiosity got the better of me and I decided to explore the school grounds. On the east side of the building was a dark spinney that ran down a steep slope to a backwater of the River Ouse. The spinney was out of bounds, but the same steep slope extended out into the playing fields, dividing the upper football pitch from a lower less even playing field. Bigger boys began grabbing some of my squealing classmates by the arms, forcing them to run backwards down the slope into a large patch of sticky mud, where a few of them ended up legs in the air, covered in dirt. Other frightened boys were held by the wrists and ankles, tossed into the air and bumped audaciously into the grass.

Seeing my impending fate, I started to run, but was rapidly caught, bringing up some of my lunch in sheer terror. The vomit deterred them for only a moment, and then I was seized by a couple of tall, mean-looking boys in green blazers who propelled me backward to the top of the slope. Grabbing my wrists, my torturers almost pulled my arms out of their sockets, as they ran like demons, dragging me to the muddy patch below. Suddenly they let go of me. I fell backwards and rolled over in the thickest area of mud. My short grey pants and new green blazer were wet and filthy. There was loud laughter and I felt horribly humiliated. After slinking away to the edge of the spinney I managed to remove some of the mud with dried grass, but for the remainder of that school day I was so miserable and uncomfortable that I almost went home. My father wrote a strong complaint to the school and received a diplomatic reply that ultimately evaded responsibility.

During the course of my school years I was to be at the receiving end of several violent acts from bullies who just felt in the mood to be aggressive. Two of them always sat together at the back of the classroom. These incidents have probably left emotional scars that make me somewhat cautious in the presence of loud, pushy individuals. Looking back, I can never be persuaded that school days are the happiest days, because for me they were the days that I felt trapped and fearful of what was to come. I felt horribly out of control and I dreamed constantly of a place where I could be safe and where people would be kind to each other. The world seemed such a wicked place, and I was to discover that some big changes were just around the corner.

Brian and Peter at the seaside in Hunstanton, Norfolk. Dad took the family every year for two weeks in a rented caravan or bungalow. We always enjoyed the amusement park.

7.

About the time that I was becoming adjusted to my new school, my father began speaking of tremendous opportunities for enterprising families in South Africa. He wrote for details of jobs in Port Elizabeth and filled our minds with stories of being able to go out in the garden and pick our own oranges and bananas, and never having to worry about the wet British climate any more. I remember feeling tremendously excited by the prospect of living in another country. I told a few friends at school that we were emigrating, and mentally I was all set to go. Then came the big disappointment.

Dad suddenly announced that he was concerned about my continuing education and that he felt unwilling to take me away from the Grammar School. Therefore he had decided to buy a shop in the nearby village of Offord Cluny. My mother would be the shopkeeper, he would continue with his daytime job, and there would be extra money for the clothes and shoes that we needed. Sadly, I listened to this change of plan, and apprehensively waited to see the new home.

Even though cars were still difficult to obtain because of post-war shortages, my father managed to purchase an old, grey Ford. Using our new mode of transport, we were taken to see the grocery store and off-licence in Offord Cluny. What an old decrepit property it looked! It had been whitewashed at the front and stood on a curve in the road between two fields. A London woman named Rose

French was the owner. She had been there for little more than a year and obviously wanted to get out fast. The property had once been a public house, and in the Deeds was referred to as "The Crown and Anchor". Beer, wine and spirits were still sold, but for consumption off the premises. The house was an L-shaped two-storey building with a sloping tiled roof covered with yellow lichen. All the downstairs rooms had uneven brick floors, and low ceilings divided by heavy black beams. There was also a beer cellar at a lower level. It separated the front sitting room from the back kitchen, necessitating a short descent and step up each time one went for meals. Upon entering the front door a rickety wooden staircase led up to four bedrooms, one being over the shop, and the other three leading straight into each other. Behind the shop on the ground floor, was another room that had a smelly, old-fashioned grate and a strange, cold atmosphere. For some reason that room always gave me the creeps because I felt some unseen presence there. In the enclosed back yard was a fully functioning water pump with a long iron handle that had to be lifted and pressed continuously for water to appear from the large grey spout. Tumbledown stables and sheds where farm implements might once have been kept surrounded the back of the property. When I enquired about the location of the toilet, I was taken down a brick path beside a building called 'the granary' and shown into a smelly outhouse where I saw what appeared to be a low table with a hole in the middle. I remember feeling disgusted by the primitive aspects of the property, upset that there was no bathroom and no instant hot water as we had enjoyed in the council house. I felt horribly cheated that my father had changed his mind and 'chickened' out on the idea of going to South Africa.

Shortly afterwards we left the town and I had the miserable task of adjusting to life in a small village, making new friends, and hearing a shop bell that rang continuously. My younger brother, Peter, appeared to enjoy assisting my father in the shop every evening. My mother would sometimes get Saturday night off and she and I would take the bus into town to visit the Hippodrome Cinema where Uncle Nigger was employed. Occasionally we had complimentary tickets and I became deeply interested in the projection of films and the collection of various filmstrips.

Our neighbours, Mr. & Mrs. Speed and their three daughters, Norma, Daphne and Jeanette lived on our right hand side, with a small field between the two properties. We first met them while exploring that field looking for walnuts that fell from a large tree.
Mrs. Speed was a short, very active lady who wore a headscarf and who, to our amazement, was not above tucking her skirt in her knickers and doing handstands against the end wall of her house, while her daughters shouted encouragement. Mrs. Speed was an extremely helpful lady, always joking and trying to shock my more straight-laced mother with her repertoire of incredible stories. Sometimes in a dramatic gesture she would actually remove her bottom dentures and pull a weird face trying to

frighten everyone by the way her lip went in and her chin stuck out. She was quite a character!

Having no bathroom, we were forced to purchase a zinc bath, which twice weekly was placed in front of the kitchen fire, filled with hot water from an old copper and used in turn by every member of the family. As a twelve-year-old boy, I had to wait for my five-year-old sister and my ten-year-old brother to precede me. After they had been dispatched to bed, I undressed and was about to step into the grey, scummy water when I heard the voice of Mrs. Speed outside the back door.

"Yoo hoo! Anyone at home?"

She knew darn well there was! She might even have peeped in at me through the kitchen window. Without further ado, she pushed upon the door and stepped inside. I scuttled into that bath quicker than I had ever done before. Mrs. Speed was smoking a cigarette and wearing the usual turban around her head.

"Let me scrub your back," she volunteered.

"I can manage," I said, demurely covering my private parts with a face flannel.

She grinned at me like a contented pussycat through the horn rimmed glasses.

"Well, don't pee in the water! Your mum's got to get in there!"

"Oh, she'll have fresh water," I retorted.

What a nerve! Yet in spite of all, I really liked the cheerful energy of Mrs. Speed. She made me laugh. She quickly disappeared down the steps into the beer cellar and up the steps the other side into the front sitting room where my mother was reading some magazines. I had just lathered up my chest and arms, and was about to rinse off when the back door suddenly opened yet again. In stepped Norma, Daphne and Jeanette.

"Is our mum here?" they chorused.

I was so astonished I could hardly speak. I mumbled something quickly, pointing in the direction of the beer cellar. The two older girls giggled and left the kitchen, but little Jeanette stared, moved closer and commented: "Our bath's bigger than that. You don't have much water, do you?"

Then she followed the others.

Such were the early days in Offord Cluny. Again I joined the church choir. The vicar was an elderly, rather boring man named Reverend Toll. One of the parishioners was a cute little dwarf lady named Mrs. Butler, who never missed a service. She lived in a small church property in the High Street, right next door to a room that was used for the Offord Cluny Sunday school. Everyone knew Mrs. Butler. She was obviously a widow, and rumour had it that she had given birth many years previously to a normal-sized daughter.

Meanwhile, my brother Peter had also passed the eleven-plus exam to attend the Grammar School, and the two of us would wait outside 'The Swan' public house every morning for the school bus to take us into town.

Copies of my early school reports are filled with comments like 'promising', 'rather slow', 'needs to pull up his socks.' In common with many children, I did much better in subjects where I really liked the teacher. I froze up completely in the presence of the woodwork master who also taught Borstal boys and was quite a bully. The gym teacher, Mr. Evans, a bald-headed man with freckles, also had a cane that he called 'Betsy', and he would occasionally swish this across the rear end of an unsuspecting boy. Needless to say, I always had a 'D' in those two subjects and showed little progress. My highest grades were surprisingly in Biology, History and Music, and the Geography teacher commented that my map work was excellent. My first 'A' was in English in July 1953. The teacher was Miss Gully. She had ginger hair, a calm personality and I related to her particularly well. The biology teacher was another favourite. She was a slim, dark-haired lady named Miss Wildeblood, who in spite of her name was most pleasant, kind and encouraging. Through all the classes I took with her I always got a 'B' and an excellent comment upon my work.

Apart from a tendency to daydream in class, there was little evidence in those days that my ultimate destiny was to be a medium, and my schooldays proved that it is not always possible to predict what a child may eventually become. Nevertheless, I believe there are many successful people in the world who were just as puzzled in *their* early days as I was, regarding the direction they should take. I now know that there are unique ways in which Heaven can help.

8.

A close, elderly neighbour, named Mrs. Wilshire was a regular customer in the shop. She smoked 'Craven A' cigarettes and was heavily addicted. She had nicotine-stained teeth and always smelled strongly of stale cat urine, but she was an accomplished pianist and expressed an interest in coaching me in singing. As we still owned the old upright piano from the days of my lessons with Mr. Dew, Mrs. Wilshire came over sometimes in the evening to play for me. I would practise singing popular songs, while my brother either left the room or discreetly held his nose in the far corner. After a while the stale cat urine was hardly noticeable.

This lonely, delightful lady, who had devoted the latter years of her life to caring for over twenty cats, was undoubtedly a generous and kind individual that the world passed by simply because she stank.

At the age of thirteen I was called upon to sing publicly at a number of local concerts, and Mrs. Wilshire was kind enough to accompany me each time. I remember strongly empathising with her loneliness as I, too, was beginning to feel alienated from my surroundings, and apart from my brother, I had no close male friends. Being useless on the football field, and totally unable to catch a ball in flight because of poor hand-eye coordination, I was not sought after by any of my peers. Therefore the chance to sing, and be publicly praised for it, was a wonderful boost to my self-esteem. I regarded Mrs. Wilshire as a true friend, and I tolerated the horrible cat odours for those very reasons. However, in the spring of nineteen fifty-two, the angelic voice broke, and my days of public singing were over. I felt miserable and awkward, unhappy with my changing body and the subtle sprouting of hair above my top lip. I went into a period of grieving over my loss of childhood and was even somewhat angry that I was growing up.

It soon became apparent by the way in which my mother hung over the kitchen sink in the mornings that something was afoot. One day, noticing her increasing size, I asked whether she was pregnant. She seldom volunteered information, as her nature was somewhat secretive, and she was obviously put out by my question.

"That's nothing to do with you," she replied rather sharply.

"But you *are*," I persisted, "or you wouldn't keep being sick."

She refused to answer my question. She seemed moody and irritable. But a few days later I had confirmation when I heard her screaming at my father in the kitchen.

"It's *your fault* I'm the way I am! I can't cope with all the work in this place! You'll have to get me some help!"

She was complaining generally about his stinginess. We still had the worn-out furniture from the Priory Road days. The window curtains looked tatty and needed replacing. We had had a bathroom created in a small workshop behind the back kitchen and a new

Raeburn stove, all of which had come from money given to my mother by Grandma Abraham. My mother rightfully resented the fact that my father had not contributed to any of these changes, kept his income secret from everybody, and the Deeds of the property were in his name alone. Years later, I realised what a horrible bone of contention this had been between them. At that time I wondered how we could possibly manage with the addition of a new baby. I remember feeling in terrible pain over the whole situation and later resolving that I would do everything in my power to make the new baby welcome and even to care for it, if necessary.

That spring I had the highest number of absences from school. Some days my mother was so unwell that she appreciated my help in the shop and in the house. I became quite domesticated, making beds each day and vacuuming the place, negotiating the piles of laundry and magazines and newspapers that my mother seemed to collect. During that time I missed so much schooling that it seriously affected my progress, leading eventually to my demotion to a lower grade in the fourth year.

September arrived and the new baby was due. The calculated date came and went. Two more weeks passed by and it seemed that the baby was reluctant to be born. My mother was taken into Paxton Park Maternity Hospital, and everyone was on tenterhooks over her condition. I took over the running of the house, preparing meals for my father and the other children. I slept badly, worried about everything, had nightmares in the tiny back bedroom

I shared with my brother, and generally felt an atmosphere of impending doom. At times I remember bursting into tears and wishing that I could escape all the problems we seemed to have after moving into the village.

A lovely baby girl was finally delivered on the early morning of the twenty-seventh, but my father hinted there had been complications and my mother was not doing well.

"She's not going to die, is she?" I asked, horrified.

"She's got something wrong with her face," he replied, awkwardly.

I was totally bewildered.

"Her face?"

"Yes. She's been paralysed down one side."

I was totally shocked.

"Oh my God!"

"The doctor says she has Bell's palsy," my father announced glumly. He explained that this was an illness involving paralysis of the facial nerves, which often caused twisting, and distortion of the features.

I was horror-stricken. My mother was going to return home, not only with a baby she had not wanted, but also with a deformed face. I immediately felt angry with God for allowing such a thing to happen, and I lost all interest in going to church. Such is the simplistic thinking of an adolescent in pain.

During the time we were waiting for my mother to return home with the baby, I had a number of rather negative dreams and psychic experiences. Twice I saw apparitions up in my parents' bedroom: grey shapes that moved across the room and disappeared through the wall. Mrs. Speed also told me that the house was alleged to be haunted by the spirit of an old man named Mr. Brown, who had once owned the property and died there. She said that the previous owners had been very frightened when they saw him on more than one occasion gliding down into the beer cellar. Perhaps he had an interest in spirits of a different kind.

I still remember the moment my mother stepped inside the front door, carrying the baby in her arms. She wore a brown hat and coat, and as she turned towards me I could not conceal my shock at the drooping left side of the mouth and the frozen eyelid. She had very little sensation on that side, and when she tried to smile at me, only the right side of her face responded.

"Oh, Mum! What have they done to you?" I couldn't help blurting out. It was too late to take back the words. She had tears in her eyes, and she had registered my shock.

Later, she explained that she had been wheeled down a draughty corridor, while in labour at the Maternity Hospital, left some time on a gurney in front of an open window, and in spite of complaining about the cold autumn wind blowing directly upon her, nothing had been done. Eventually in the labour ward she had gone through excruciating pain with a breech delivery. It was obviously all too much for her shattered system. She never got pregnant again.

The doctor later urged my father to sue the Maternity Hospital for negligence, and my mother was sent for regular heat treatment and speech therapy. At night she had to close her left eyelid with her finger. She had difficulty speaking certain words. She was badly disfigured and there was clearly a good case for legal action.

I wanted justice for my mother because I was angry over the whole thing. No amount of money can compensate you for the loss of your looks, and my mother had been an extremely pretty woman. Legal aid would have been available, but my father did not wish to disclose his assets, and as the case would obviously have been contested, he was fearful of losing all his precious savings on legal fees. He wrote a number of letters to the Department of Health, but no one would assume responsibility. Consequently nothing was done. I believe that this was one of the supreme spiritual tests that my father had to undergo. He should have put the love of his wife before anything else. In my humble opinion, I feel that if he had truly put his mind to getting justice for my mother, it would have strengthened his marriage and put all of us in a better financial situation. Even the family doctor had said that the case was a clear-cut one of medical negligence. But my father was obviously not ready to take on that supreme challenge. It pains me to write this and I hope he will forgive me for these comments.

9.

Upon my demotion to Form 4B at school, I found myself with a collection of adolescents who seemed more relaxed, cheerful and friendly. Our new form teacher was Mr. Kenneth Brown, the music master of the school. He was a disciplinarian, but he did it with a great sense of humour. He was a skinny man with buckteeth, somewhat tousled brown hair and bright brown eyes that appeared owl-like through the horn-rimmed glasses he wore. There were times when he could be incredibly funny. He led the school choir and would play a large grand piano during morning assembly, turning towards us and grinning with his buckteeth in a mischievous manner. When we were due for dismissal from the assembly hall, he would make us stand up quietly and wait for our turn. Then he would humorously insult us:

"Come on! Stand up straight! Stop swaying about like ears of corn, you foolish Fenland turnips!"

He was constantly reminding us that we were the products of an agricultural area. Nevertheless, we all loved him!

Having rejected the Church of England as being altogether too mournful and depressing, I began to seek knowledge in alternative areas. A second hand bookshop produced something on Astrology and Palmistry, and I became an avid reader of such literature. I took one book to school and read out some of the descriptions of the zodiac signs to some of my classmates, who lapped this up with great enthusiasm, and my popularity improved.

As much as I hated organised games, Mr. Brown inspired me to take part in cross-country running. A tall boy named Nelson Roderick Davies would often accompany me. His mother also ran a village post office and general store, so we had that much in common. He seemed to like me and we hung out together. Roy (as he preferred to be known), was an excellent runner and was somewhat self-conscious about his height. He would talk about different girls that he fancied and the two of us managed to wangle entrance into an early 'X'-rated movie at the local cinema. In those days the most you saw was a brief shot of bare breasts. A woman did a not-very-daring striptease on screen, and Roy joked about the front of his pants that responded accordingly. He was a good friend to me and we shared many laughs together. Roy (God bless him) died in a tragic car accident some years later, not long after his marriage. I have sometimes felt the spiritual presence of this tall, friendly boy, and think of him with great affection. His birth sign was Aries and he understood me very well.

Later that year I also became better acquainted with another classmate whose parents lived in Huntingdon. He was Alan Clayton. He was unable to play games because he suffered from asthma. He was a quiet boy, tall and well-built with soft, blue eyes and a longish, oval face. I discovered that his birth sign was also Aries! His mother worked in a sweet factory and he referred to her as 'red hot momma.' He soon invited me to his home where his slim, cheerful mother took an interest in my amateur piano playing and made me feel most welcome. The situation in my own home was so stressed and painful that I think I was trying to belong to a family that was relatively happy. Roy had begun courting by this time, so consequently I saw less of him, and Alan became the new best friend. As all adolescents know, a best friend is terribly important. It is someone who accepts you as you are, listens to your problems with sympathy and tries to help you. I found Alan to be particularly kind and understanding with an offbeat sense of humour and good moral standards. As our friendship developed, we found we could discuss many topics on quite a deep level. I had been reading books about haunted houses, poltergeists and Astrology, and Alan was an admirable sounding board for all this. I confided in him that I had seen apparitions at home, and they had somewhat disturbed me. He also knew that I was feeling quite miserable living with my arguing parents. The teenage Angst had fully descended.

One weekend, when I was staying at Alan's house in Huntingdon, we discussed the subject of telepathy, and decided to experiment with this. Sitting in opposite chairs, we took turns at sending and receiving. On a few occasions Alan was able to accurately tune in to my thoughts, but by far the greatest success occurred when I was the receiver. Repeatedly, I was able to describe his thoughts in detail, and he was quite amazed by my accuracy. This was all very new and exciting. We spoke about developing a stage act and possibly making a lot of money doing demonstrations of mind reading. 'Red hot momma' thought it was fun and encouraged us both in these games. I envied Alan his relatively carefree home and supportive parents. But his life was not to remain untroubled for long.

Mr. Clayton, who had worked as a gardener for many years, suddenly passed away, and Alan's mother decided to leave the town and move closer to her family in Northamptonshire. Alan followed and the friendship continued by correspondence and long cycle rides over to the next county. I badly needed his opinion on many things. He was the first friend I had ever known who was able to transmit such clear and unmistakable images into my mind. We are still in contact to this day, although many miles apart.

Soon began one of the darkest times of my adolescence. I felt trapped in the old run-down village property. I began to hate the shop that demanded my constant attention. I was ashamed of the furniture and acutely aware of my mother's inability to cope with the demands of the house, business and a new baby. I remember having several blitzes on the living room, clearing out piles of old newspapers and other stuff my mother had collected. It was really quite difficult as I had little support in my attempts to keep the place looking decent. I think my parents were both 'packrats,' survivors of the wartime 'it might come in useful' mentality.

Throughout all this turmoil the new baby, christened Wendy Ann behaved like a little angel. She hardly ever cried. She was one of the best babies I had ever encountered. I grew much attached to her and often carried her around in my arms. Later, when she began talking, she had rather a low voice and a cute way of copying what was said. Years have gone by and sadly she passed into spirit in 2017 as a result of ovarian cancer. She was a talented musician, directed a choir in Birmingham, England and had many friends. She had also taught school and been a psychological counsellor in a doctor's office. We all miss you, Wendy and are proud of your achievements. Being the last of the siblings to arrive and the first to leave planet Earth we know that you are very special and will continue doing good things in the world of spirit.

During my fifth year at Grammar School, I was feeling so very depressed, awkward and anxious about myself that I decided to seek the help of a psychiatrist. I frequently heard voices in my head, a few of which gave me helpful directions, like telling me the location of mushrooms in the fields, but some of the voices were dark and depressing, suggesting that I was useless and that I should kill myself. At one point I came dangerously close to taking a bottle of pills, as I was feeling so alienated from everything. Fortunately logic prevailed, and I managed to live with the depression and ultimately to overcome it.

I saw the psychiatrist for about twenty minutes once a month at the local hospital. I was still much too shy and inhibited to really tell him everything as I felt guilty to implicate my hardworking parents in any way, but somehow we got through the brief sessions. The psychiatrist thought I was a late developer and not aggressive enough. He decided to give me small doses of hormones to improve my energy level and speed my entry into manhood. The pills, which I had to dissolve under my tongue, appeared to work for a time, giving me more energy, an enhanced libido and a greater sense of being in control, though my mother complained at the time that I was argumentative and difficult to live with. I was on those pills for almost a year before I realised that they were not the answer, and that they might even have harmful side effects. My problem was a mental and spiritual one, and had more to do with my environment than my physical body.

At this time I began reading books on health and diet, and announced to my shocked parents that I was no longer going to eat meat, as I hated the idea of animals being slaughtered. This caused quite a commotion, but my wishes were finally respected, and some years later my young sister Wendy also became a vegetarian. Much later in life my other sister Joy also followed suit.

Throughout this awkward, adolescent period I had a most wonderful friend in my father's younger sister, Doreen. She was always so pleasant and supportive to me when I was down. 'Dorry' as I called her, ran a second-hand clothing shop in the nearby town of St. Ives and later in Huntingdon. She was in partnership with one of the most extraordinary and loveable women I have ever met – a divorced woman named Nora Remes, who had a young football-loving son named Carlos. Nora, always known affectionately as 'Remie' had red hair, a wiry body and thin face and bore a superficial resemblance to the actress Marlene Dietrich. Remie was dramatic, funny and always game for a practical joke. She once told me "My parents were both cousins, so that's probably why I'm such an odd bod!" She was born a few minutes before midnight on March 31st, so always joked that she just missed being an April fool! I spent many a side-splitting hour with this amazing and loveable lady who had a natural gift for storytelling, and much later in my life Remie proved to be highly supportive to me in my work as a medium. Both she and Dorry were interested in Spiritualism and at that time they shared a home in the town. They seemed to know everybody. Their business, known as 'Noreen's Dress Agency' was a combination of both their names. Noreen's was opposite a bank, which had a large plate glass window. At one end of the window the Manager could be seen sitting in his office. The mischievous Remie would often stand in her own window, and in the process of decorating it would wave frilly underwear, corsets and other extraordinary garments as the rather sedate manager stared in her direction.

"I love to see the expression on his face!" she said, gleefully, "His eyes pop out like organ stops!"

Remie was also fond of carrying a piece of artificial dog poop in her bag and quietly depositing the brown, curly object on a dog-owner's freshly-cleaned carpet. My mother had this trick played upon her. Remie could keep an extremely straight face as she pointed and yelled "Oh Betty! Look what the dog has done!"

We were at that time the new owners of a beautiful black Labrador retriever named 'Trixie.' Trixie looked up at us with a hurt expression, made a funny little noise and promptly trotted out of the room. My mother was about to clean up the light brown curly piece of poop when Remie said "Oh never mind! I'll get rid of it." When she picked it up and popped it in her handbag, we all burst out laughing.

The point of describing these two important people in my life is that they were the first ones to actually talk to me about *physical mediums*. People like me who hear the thoughts of the dead are known technically as *mental mediums,* but there are other kinds of mediums who are able to be used by the spirit scientists for the production of physical phenomena. Those *physical mediums* are the ones sought out by scientists in our world, as such phenomena can, at certain times, be photographed, recorded, and if observed honestly, provide evidence of the reality of a spiritual realm. It was Dorry and Remie who first initiated me into the extraordinary séance room of Mrs. Ann Copley, a local medium who never charged a penny for her services.

"Ann is a physical medium," Dorry explained, "She produces the voices of the spirits right in the air in front of you."

I was totally bewildered and really thought that my kind aunt was being horribly deceived.

"Couldn't this be trickery?"

"No," Dorry asserted, "My brother Frank came through and told me things that only he and I knew about."

Dorry also told me how, many years ago, she had lost a very dear teenage friend named Madge Benstead. Madge had died at the Papworth Sanatorium in Cambridgeshire from tuberculosis. Dorry's own mother had also died of the same disease. Madge Benstead had apparently come through and spoken in Ann Copley's séance room, though Ann knew nothing of Madge. This information blew my mind. Dorry was a very truthful and honest lady with an educated and pleasant speaking voice. I knew that she would not lie to me and that she was not stupid. I wanted to know more about this extraordinary communication. I had so many questions that needed answers. How could dead people who no longer possessed a physical body speak in the air and be tape-recorded by those present? It sounded as though my loving aunt was the victim of an absurd hoax, but what could possibly be the motive, as no money was exchanged? I was deeply puzzled by all this and decided that it was time to make a serious investigation of the subject called Spiritualism.

Above: Aunt Dorry with her business partner Nora Remes who was a natural born comedian. With Sun in Aries, Moon in Leo and Capricorn rising, Remie knew how to make friends with all the right people. Both she and Dorry were most kind and generous to me.

Above: Ann Copley with poodle, Dorry, myself and Bob Copley.

10.

During my last two years in the sixth form at school, I began attending the Huntingdon Spiritualist Church. I borrowed books from the church library and began to investigate the mysteries of mediumship. It was the beginning of one of the greatest adventures of my life.

At that time the Huntingdon Spiritualist Church held its meetings in a long, wooden barn-like building that was also used by the Red Cross. That was where I first became acquainted with a tall, silvery-haired, balding man named Robert Alvery Copley. He turned out to be the husband of the very Ann Copley my aunt had mentioned. Mr. Copley was the leader of the band of spiritual healers at the church. He was also involved with the local Red Cross and St. John's Ambulance groups, and he was a wealthy and well-known lawyer in the county. Like his father before him he was deeply involved in Spiritualism. He often stood on the church platform and gave trance addresses in which the spirit of a North American Indian was said to be overshadowing him. I remember one particular address in which he railed against some of the orthodox medical profession and the ways in which they pushed drugs upon the unsuspecting people, making them wholly dependent upon medications, and afraid to take an active part in their own healing by changing their diet or using more natural methods. It made good sense to me. I watched Mr. Copley giving healing to people in pain and was amazed by the way in which the pain was usually relieved. Something that impressed me strongly at the time was the essential kindness of all the church members. A tiny lady named Mary Wonnacott, jokingly referred to by another church member as "Mrs. One O'clock", played the organ. She had a very sweet angelic face. People came and talked with me as though they cared, and it was obvious that they were sensitive to my feelings as an enquiring adolescent. I felt that I had found an 'extended family' and I began making regular Sunday evening visits to this warm and friendly place.

For the first time at school I really began to enjoy the English, History and Geography I was taking as main subjects. I wriggled out of games and PE totally. I just didn't show up. Undoubtedly my favourite teacher was Mrs. Mary Stuart, the senior mistress who took us for A-level English. Although she walked with a slight limp, she was energetic and charming. Her short, greying hair was drawn back into a bun. She had a round face, a small hooked nose and the brightest of china-blue eyes. Mrs. Stuart kept the discussions lively and interesting. Her warmth and natural wisdom were like a breath of fresh air, and she was a wonderful teacher. I loved and adored this woman. She had vast knowledge, and as we studied the English Romantic Poets I found my own creativity blossoming in the form of numerous poems which I scribbled on every available scrap of paper. I used the intricate rhyme schemes of Keats and Shelley. I experimented with the sonnet and the elegy. I tried to follow Keats' advice and 'load every rift with ore', and then I tried my hand at satire. The outcome was a long, humorous poem describing every teacher at the school. I read it out to the Sixth Form Society, in the presence of Mr. Rowntree and Mrs. Stuart. The audience laughed, clapped and cheered, and it was suggested that the poem be published in the school magazine; but later, upon analysis, it was thought that outsiders reading the poem might misunderstand the satire and give some of the teachers a hard time. So it was never published. Mr. Rowntree, however, did write me a brief note in which he expressed his enjoyment of the humour, but said he was going to keep a copy of the poem to use in evidence against me!

The upper sixth English class held in the library. Extreme left is Mary Stuart. The author is third from left.

During my final year at school, *'East of Eden'* and *'Rebel without a Cause'* played at the Hippodrome Cinema in town. I was totally mesmerised by the performances of James Dean. He suddenly became my hero. I sat up late one night and wrote an Elegy upon his death, and later I sent this poem to the national magazine '*Picture Post*', which published several stanzas in an article about the James Dean cult. I was not paid anything for my poem, but felt proud that a piece of my writing had appeared in such a prestigious magazine.

I began corresponding with an American schoolteacher named Evelyn H. Hunt, who lived in Woodstock, Vermont. She had also written poems on the death of James Dean, and she was kind enough to send me several copies. I confided in her about my frustration at home, and found her to be a much better psychiatrist than the one I had visited. I will always remember this gracious lady who took the trouble to give advice and reassurance to a lonely and troubled adolescent.

During this time of study and stress I became even more alienated from my parents. My mother was constantly complaining about my father and trying to draw me into taking sides, which was particularly painful. I liked my father. He was an industrious man and he had become a teacher of shorthand and typewriting, doing his evening classes in town after he had already worked a nine-to-five office job. The extra money he earned was carefully banked in his own name, which was probably the cause of my mother's dissatisfaction. Meanwhile the rest of us were left to take care of the shop. There was a horrible lack of communication and we were dangerously close to becoming a dysfunctional family.

I owned a small boat at the time. I kept my boat tied to a willow tree in a brook that led directly into the River Ouse. I spent many hours alone on the river during the summer, observing the moorhens and other fowl and often I would plunge into the cold water and have a swim, later drying off on the river bank. I was a skinny youth with mushroom-white flesh and I was horribly self-conscious about my body.

Upon leaving school I should have accepted my father's offer to send me to college. Instead I tried a short spell in an architect's office on the Market Square, helped to survey houses and take measurements, but as I was promised remuneration for my services and never received it, I quit that job. Knowing that I was unemployed, Uncle Nigger had a unique suggestion. He had married Mrs. Eva Ashpole, the widowed landlady of 'The Market Inn', a well-known Huntingdon pub, and my uncle came into contact with many American servicemen from the local US Base. He learned that they were seeking a bartender at the Officers' Club, and he suggested that I apply for this position. I did so, and to my surprise was accepted. After chest X-rays and blood tests I started work every evening at the Officers' Club in Alconbury. I knew nothing about the mixing of drinks, but somehow I learned and survived the smoky atmosphere and the loud music from the jukebox. It was the height of the rock and roll period, with Bill Haley and his Comets blasting everybody's eardrums. It was quite fun to receive tips in American money and also to be able to spend it on fried egg sandwiches and American cookies. The men in the bar were basically decent to me, as I was "just a young kid." However, within a month I was informed that they could no longer employ me because I had to be twenty-one by US law. A tall, friendly guy named Sergeant Chuck Bennett offered me a job as a batman at the Bachelors' Official Quarters for five pounds a week. I had to take care of the premises, polish the floor and clean the men's rooms and the bathrooms. I accepted Sergeant Bennett's offer.

Each day I cycled about sixteen miles through wind and rain and snow. It was winter time and quite cold. I had no money to buy a car, and like most boys of my age, I was not qualified to drive. I was fascinated by the lives of the American airmen on the Base. Everyone seemed friendly and the job was not too demanding. A couple of other Englishmen were employed in the adjoining buildings and we took our coffee breaks together.

On one occasion an extremely pleasant, dark-haired man with wideset grey eyes joined us. He was introduced as Mr. Donald Damer. He was a civilian and he taught mathematics at the Base School.
He told me he was making a study of the English poets of the First World War. He particularly liked Wilfred Owen and Rupert Brooke. I showed him some of the poems I had written and was surprised when he expressed a genuine admiration for my style and use of vocabulary. He told me that he also loved music and visited London frequently to attend operas at Covent Garden. He said he was dating an

English girl but he was unsure where the relationship was going. Don and I became very good friends. He was in his late twenties and talked frankly to me about his disillusionment with life in the States and his search for a more peaceful life-style in Europe. Occasionally he drove over to my home in his little Volkswagen beetle car, picked me up and we would make a circular tour of the neighbouring villages, talking constantly about writers and poets and the state of the world. I was pleased that this well-educated and genuinely nice man should find me worthy of his companionship. Don seemed to be a natural philosopher. We had a great deal in common. We shared the same birth month (His birthday was March 21st). He gave up time to be with me and obviously liked me as a person. Don later told me of his break-up with the English girl, and that he was contemplating entering a monastery. He seemed to be going through a spiritual crisis and I felt powerless to help him. Years later I understood that many young Americans went through a natural aversion to their country's involvement in the Korean War and later in the Vietnam War. They wanted no part of it, let alone to be conscripted. Perhaps that was one of Don's basic fears and why he was teaching school in Europe. Many years later I wrote a positive scenario for my friend when I put him as a character in my first novel 'Some go Haunting.' Don became the American school-teacher who helped solve a reincarnation mystery. His character and personality fitted the part ideally.

11.

Just before accepting the batman's job on the Alconbury Air Base, I had written a letter to the owner of a Cambridge bookstore enquiring whether there was any prospect of work. Almost two months later I received a positive reply. I went for an interview and was given a job as assistant salesman on the ground floor of Deighton Bell in Trinity Street. As there was no direct bus service from Offord Cluny, my Aunt Dorry suggested that I stay with her in the property she had purchased on the Market Square at the nearby town of St. Neots, where there was a direct bus service into Cambridge.

Red-haired Remie had dissolved her business partnership with Dorry and had moved to Deal in Kent to be near a gentleman friend. My grandfather Hurst's second wife, Auntie Mary, had died of cancer the previous year, so grandfather had sold his bungalow where I had enjoyed many weekends and was now living with his daughter at the Market Square property. I accepted Dorry's kind offer of accommodation with considerable relief. I packed my few belongings into an old suitcase and Dorry came to pick me up at the Offord Cluny shop. My mother was upset and cried, but I felt as though a great burden had been lifted from my shoulders, as I had always hated living in that place. At least my parents would have one less mouth to feed, and I would be earning just enough to get by on my own.

I sometimes wonder whether that old village property was haunted by some undesirable entities and whether, in my rage and vulnerability, I had become at times a human sounding board for their dark thoughts. Once while deep digging the back garden I found a rusted flintlock pistol and my imagination ran wild! Had someone back in the eighteenth century been murdered on the property and the weapon buried. As the place had once been an old tavern, who knows what dramas had been enacted within its walls! As soon as I left the place, the greyness and depression seemed to clear away like magic. I began to feel like a brand new person.

Dorry proved to be a wonderful, lifelong friend. She had kind, brown eyes and a calm soothing manner. She was a Libra and liked to have a balanced life. She never screamed at me or told me what to do, yet we always discussed things rationally and found ourselves agreeing on most points. She gave me a tremendous amount of information about her experiences in the Spiritualist Movement and how it was necessary to question everything that came through and use our own judgement regarding the messages from the other side.

"The spirits' sense of timing is not always correct," she explained, "because they are living in a different dimension from us, and we can also change our minds about things and take a different course from the one expected. That's why I believe the future is not fixed. We can definitely change it."

Then she said something I will never forget:

"Brian, I do believe that you could be a very good medium! You have that kind of sensitivity."

Dorry was most perceptive!

Meanwhile I had started my job in the Cambridge bookstore and I had so much to learn. The Manager was a short grey-haired man with bulging eyes and a quick temper. He would strut energetically about, put on a 'posh voice' with some of the professors, and he was obviously impatient with an inexperienced teenager. There was also a thin, dark-haired woman who arrived late every morning, stuttered, had pencilled eyebrows, and who regarded me with contempt. I was soon transferred down in the basement with an elderly man named Mr. Papworth, who was much easier to get along with.

During my lunch hour I would try to explore some of the back streets of Cambridge, and I usually found myself eating at a self-service restaurant in the old Petty Cury. It was there that I met a sweet lady with a short pageboy hairstyle. She was smartly dressed and told me that she was employed in a drapery store. We often shared a table and I learned that Nora had recently separated from her bullying husband. She asked whether I had seen the Cambridge Botanical Gardens, and of course I had not. We arranged a weekend visit to the beautiful orchid houses, and while admiring the curves and colours of Nature's paint box, Nora confided how happy she was to be in my company. It almost seemed like we had known each other in a past life. I was a gauche young boy barely nineteen, and she was a married woman twenty years older. Nora had a 'little girl' quality that was very appealing. She told me her birth sign was Leo. We became good friends and I spent many hours in her company. We often visited the Fitzwilliam Museum where I enjoyed gazing at some of the world's great paintings. On our visits there we both became acquainted with a charming elderly gentleman who had been employed there for some years. He was known as 'Dixie' Dean. He would smile at us in a fatherly manner, point out particular paintings to us and tell us little anecdotes about the artists. I was particularly interested in Stanley Spencer's churchyard paintings with their vivid colours and bizarre figures, and Mr. Dean would stand beside us, gazing thoughtfully through his glasses, and make witty remarks. I wish all museum personnel were as interested in their visitors as dear Mr. Dean. He was a lovely old gentleman who made every museum visit a pleasure. He must have died long ago, but his round, benevolent face and mischievous chuckle are still imprinted clearly upon my mind.

Back in St. Neots it was clear that Aunt Dorry was unwell. She began to lose a lot of weight. She developed a hacking cough and the normal colour in her cheeks disappeared. Grandfather's pipe and cigars, which he would smoke continuously in the downstairs room, bothered everyone. Eventually the doctor was called in and Dorry was taken to hospital. X-rays revealed that she had contracted tuberculosis, exactly as her mother had done, and preparations were made for her admission to Papworth Sanatorium where her dear friend Madge Benstead had died in June, 1938. The Market Square property had to be sold, grandfather was admitted to a nearby retirement home, and I had to move out of the attic bedsitter I had occupied. In hospital, large amounts of fluid were drained from Dorry's lungs. She was confined to bed, put on antibiotics and was told that the process of healing would take at least two years. I was shocked, grieved and hurt that this wonderful lady, who had been such a kind and supportive friend, should have to deal with this life-threatening situation. It just didn't seem fair.

I went into lodgings with a Mr. & Mrs. Fisher at Girton village, just outside Cambridge. The husband was a redheaded engineer and the wife a doctor, though she was not practising. They were very pleasant to me and Mrs. Fisher always cooked a good dinner for me in the evening. I cycled to work each day, mingling with the undergraduates, wishing at times that I could be one of their numbers. Donald Damer visited me at Girton, bringing with him an LP record of Beethoven's Pastoral Symphony (which I still possess). He told me he was leaving England in order to teach at a Base school in Germany. I made English tea for him, told him how much I would miss him, and gave him details of my aunt's terrible illness. Finally we hugged each other and I knew inwardly that I would not see him again. We had shared so many interests, and his friendship had been so good that I felt quite sad to see him go. I am sure that my loss was someone else's gain. He was a very special kind of person with unique insight and great empathy for the suffering of others.

About that time I began to feel the old depression and darkness returning. Then one day in Cambridge I was stung on the right hand by a wasp. The sting turned septic and I developed a high fever and a painful swelling which had to be lanced at the hospital. My kind landlady, Mrs. Fisher, although a doctor herself, was not legally authorised to take care of me, but she drove me back to Offord Cluny where I stayed with my family for several weeks until I recovered.

During my time back at the old village property I found myself becoming quite introspective and superstitious. I wondered whether the sting was a sign that I should get out of Cambridge. As much as I loved the city, I had begun to find the bookshop work boring and unrewarding. Then my father's brother Noel, and his wife Blanche, visited us in the village. They had been to see Dorry in the sanatorium at Papworth. At that time they had a flat in Brixton, South London, and it was suggested that I might like to visit them and look for a job in the big city. It was obvious to me that the time was ripe for further changes, and shortly afterwards, I quit my job at the bookstore, said goodbye to Nora and joined my aunt and uncle in Brixton. For a long time I carried around a load of guilt about hurting Nora. We had had a brief love affair and I had responded to her sweet and gentle personality, but the age difference seemed too great for me to continue the relationship, and she was so vulnerable. Seeing her distressed condition, I decided never to get involved with any woman again unless I felt it was the real thing. I hated the pain I had caused her and felt awful about leaving for London, but the move proved to be a significant turning point in my life.

Exciting developments were about to take place, and I was to meet some important people who were major influences in my later work for Spiritualism.

Above: Dorry and I loved clowning around. She had a wonderful sense of humour and enjoyed a glass of beer at the local pub. She helped me through my severe depression and will always be loved for it.

12.

I had not seen much of Uncle Noel since I had welcomed him home from the war at my grandfather's bungalow. Noel was the blonde member of the family. He was muscular and well-built and gifted with a powerful singing voice. He had sung at community concerts and also in church. His rendition of '*Ave Maria*' had brought tears to many eyes. He also sang '*Love is a Many-Splendored Thing*' and a hauntingly beautiful number entitled '*Somewhere a Voice is Calling.*' In addition to this he could yodel as well as any Swiss mountaineer. After his release from Germany as a prisoner-of-war he had tried to earn a living in the London nightclubs. London had suffered badly in the blitz and consequently there were a limited number of locations that would employ a handsome and talented unknown. He got his break when he auditioned for the chorus in a new production of 'Annie Get Your Gun', which was to open at the London Coliseum and star Bill Johnson and Dolores Gray. Noel was among the lucky applicants, and later our father was able to take us to London to see our popular uncle dance, and appear in a number of crowd scenes, in a variety of costumes from a tuxedo to a cowboy outfit. Noel was a Leo, of course and a natural for the stage. We were very proud of him. Later, my talented uncle was to encounter a chubby, round-faced man with sleek dark hair, who was looking for a partner in a comedy nightclub act. The two of them tried out a few routines, the chubby man liked my uncle and they consequently played together at a number of nightclubs in the West End. When my uncle left show business to get married, the round-faced man went on to become one of the naughtiest comedians that England has ever known. He was none other than the irrepressible Benny Hill! Many years later, Noel took me to meet Benny at the Shepherds Bush studios in London. Backstage, Benny was bubbling with energy and Noel and he engaged in some quick-fire repartee, to the amusement of all present. But I am jumping ahead of my story.

When I joined Noel and Blanche, he was working for the Watneys Brewery and she was employed as a furrier in Oxford Circus. Her prestigious firm specialised in fur coats for various members of the royal family, including Princess Margaret. Blanche was often called upon to be a stand-in for coat fittings for the princess as they were both about the same height and build. Blanche was from an East London family and was half Jewish. She was a little older than my uncle and sometimes teased him about it. She would wave her finger in the air, circle around him and comment:

"I don't know what he'd do without me! He knows when he's well off, don't you Noel?"

He nicknamed her 'Dolly', and the two of them had little comic routines that they went through together in their lively and sparkling relationship. There was never a dull moment in Brixton Road. I wished my own parents could have been as happy.

Within a short time I had got a jack-of-all-trades job with a Victoria Street theatre ticket agency. I had to run errands with theatre and sports events tickets, and the bonus was being able to get into many of the shows free of charge. My appetite for the theatre was really whetted. One of the exciting events I attended was the opening night of 'My Fair Lady' at Drury Lane Theatre. I sat way up in the gallery but with opera glasses I could still enjoy the wonderful music, costumes and colourful sets of that amazing show. A couple of years later I actually worked at Drury Lane, selling programmes and ice cream and was able to enjoy the music nightly.

Noel and Blanche were kindness itself. I was very happy staying with them because there was never any fighting and they obviously loved each other dearly. Noel would entertain us with stories about his days in show business and occasionally he would refer to his time as a prisoner-of-war. He said that he enjoyed his food and his wine all the more when he remembered those wartime days behind barbed wire on a starvation diet.

Within a couple of months I had found myself a bed-sitter a little further down the Brixton Road. The pleasant landlady, Mrs. Clifton, told me that I would have to share with another boy. I was hoping to rent the small room at the top, but I was told that a film extra named Ted Glennon occupied this.
"The room might be available later," Mrs. Clifton promised. So I accepted the shared room with the twin beds. My roommate was a tall, thin boy with buckteeth and large glasses. We had nothing in

common, as the only topic of conversation was his work at the soup factory and how he hated reading books. He obviously found an ex-grammar schoolboy equally boring and within a few weeks he was gone.

Mrs. Clifton then announced the arrival of a music student who would like to share the room with me. He was a smiling-faced, chubby, English/Italian boy who had been born in Peterborough, quite close to my own neck of the woods. In walked Geoffrey Keay. He wore a large black-and-white cable-knit sweater that made his ample chest look even larger. He greeted me in a pleasant baritone voice, shook hands with genuine warmth and seemed delighted that I was a native of his own area. I immediately liked this genial Pisces boy. Soon he was telling me about his studies at the London Guildhall School of Music and Drama and how he wanted to be an opera singer. I listened with rapt attention. Geoffrey loved to eat Italian food, and it was he who taught me the correct manner of twisting my spaghetti round a fork while holding it steady with a spoon. The most important information that he gave me, however, was that the London County Council had money to spare and was giving Grants to promising students who might wish to attend the Guildhall School. When he heard that I worked in the theatre ticket business, he suggested that I might apply to the London County Council for a Grant to be a drama student.

"Geoffrey, you're a genius!" I said, "What a wonderful idea!"

And it was. I auditioned at County Hall on the south bank of the River Thames, performed a small scene I had written myself, also recited one of my own poems, to the obvious delight of the female adjudicator and I quickly heard that I was the recipient of a major county award. I was overwhelmed with excitement that at last I could go to college and have the opportunity of meeting artistic and creative young people who wanted to better their stations in this challenging world. Geoffrey Keay came into my life at exactly the right moment, and I will always be deeply grateful to my opera-singing friend for his timely suggestion. Although he now lives in Italy where he nursed his beautiful wife, Toni through a long and fatal illness we remain in touch.

13.

It was not so strange that I was drawn to the theatre. During my time in the sixth form at school I had played the gloomy Jacques in *Shakespeare's 'As You Like It'*. I was dressed all in black and apparently electrified the audience with my rendition of 'All the world's a stage.' I had a good write-up on the front page of the *Hunts Post,* and they thought I was ideal for the part. Perhaps it was because I was feeling so miserable at the time! Now I had received a major grant to study dramatic art.

At that time The Guildhall School of Music and Drama was in John Carpenter Street, on the north bank of the River Thames, just south of the newspaper world of Fleet Street. The building looked rather like a bank on the outside. Most of the music students took their classes in upstairs rooms behind double glass doors, in order to insulate the rest of the building from the squeals of off-key violins and booming trumpets. The drama department was mostly on the ground floor and in the basement with occasional use of upstairs rooms for mime and movement and literature classes. The cafeteria was where everyone gathered to gossip.

My first private professor was Mr. Rex Walters who was an excellent teacher, but somewhat disinterested and impatient if he did not see immediate talent. I worked to the best of my ability but obviously did not possess the pizzazz and confidence that he was looking for. He had expressed an opinion to me that it was a questionable use of the taxpayers' money to give grants to drama students. When I did not make the rapid progress he expected, he was mean enough to try and get my grant withdrawn. The lady at County Hall suggested I change my private professor and just keep my nose to the grindstone. Her suggestion proved to be a wise one. I was put under the tuition of Mr. Daniel Roberts, a delightful elderly man with half-moon glasses, who succeeded in giving me confidence and fostering my love of poetry and drama. 'Danny', as all his students affectionately knew him, told me that I was a 'good person' and he felt sure that I would accomplish something worthwhile in the world. He was a lover of the works of Anton Chekhov and allowed me to produce a scene from *The Three Sisters* for the term drama project. I am eternally grateful to 'Danny' for his basic kindness and skill in steering me in the right direction. A devout Roman Catholic, 'Danny' nevertheless was supportive of my interest in Spiritualism. He was something like a father confessor and because of his gentle wisdom was adored by the students.

For the first time in my life I was surrounded by a number of really friendly and warm young people who seemed to accept my unusual interests without batting an eyelid. I calculated horoscope charts for a number of my classmates, helped them with relationship problems and gave them free readings. One young man who wore a brown sweater with a yellow zigzag pattern asked me, in a voice that betrayed a North Country working class origin, to prepare a chart for him. I remember telling him that he had a strong likelihood of achieving fame in adventurous and dramatic roles in television. He had an amused scepticism at the time, as he did not have the features of the classic leading man, but was endowed with a thin face, pointed chin and rather penetrating eyes. He cleaned offices to earn money to pay for his studies, and seemed the least likely to become a successful star. His name was John Noakes, and later he did star in the famous BBC *Blue Peter* series, where he demonstrated mountaineering, hang gliding and just about every other dangerous pursuit for our instruction and entertainment. My prediction for John proved to be right on the money!

Other contemporaries of mine at the Guildhall School were Rosalie Crutchley, Alan Bates, Murray Melvin and the dramatic actress Katy Wild, who later appeared as a deaf and dumb girl in Hammer Film Company's *Evil of Frankenstein*. Katy also had a small role in *Dr. Terror's House of Horrors*, and starred in another movie about killer bees. Katy's real name was Jacqueline Marygold, and her lively personality and enthusiasm made her a good producer at the Guildhall. I appeared in a couple of her scenes and enjoyed working with her.

Meanwhile, back at Brixton Road, the genial Geoffrey Keay had moved out to be with some Italian friends. He had met a serious young

Capricorn lady who was later to become his devoted wife. Ted, the tall film extra who lived in the upstairs room, became friendlier when he knew I was studying drama. He had been working as Burt Lancaster's stand-in on a movie and had also appeared in a saloon bar scene in a ridiculous Western comedy spoof entitled *The Sheriff of Fractured Jaw*. Ted was an auburn-haired Yorkshire man of Irish ancestry, who later had a successful career as a physiotherapist. He sensed my need of a friend and took me exploring the bohemian Soho area of London, and especially some of the coffee bars.

"This is where you can really study human nature," he commented.

One Soho coffee bar went by the delightful name of *Heaven and Hell*. The décor upstairs was blue and white, with angels floating around playing harps, but in the basement it was menacing and gloomy, with dull, red lighting, coffins for tables, tombstones and ghouls with deep glaring eyes. All kinds of extraordinary people went there for conversation and companionship. Perhaps there was drug taking, but I never saw it. I had no interest in messing up my mind with illegal substances. In another coffee bar there sat a pleasant-natured, but physically dirty man by the name of Ernest Page. He had long, shoulder-length white hair and a beard, and he always sat in the corner with a suitcase full of Astrological Ephemerides. For a cup of lemon tea and/or a shilling he would advise you on the current planetary transits. He spoke with an educated voice, and said he had once been a Post Office worker who had scoffed at Astrology. Later, through careful investigation, he had become converted, decided to devote the rest of his life to its study, and to give up his day job. As a result, he slept in doorways, abandoned buildings or relied upon the kindness of strangers. Ernest gave me some very accurate information as he read my birth chart. He warned me that if I married at all, it should not be until much later in life, as Moon conjunct Mars in the seventh house square Pluto was not indicative of a fortunate early relationship.

"Your marriage house is badly afflicted," he said, "You'd be better off just living with someone. Your horoscope tells me that you could be a very good medium."

There it was again, the prediction that I would have psychic ability. Years later I thought of his words when a brief marriage ended abruptly. Ernest was featured in a film documentary about Soho nightlife, and I was informed some years later, that he had died while travelling in Europe. Under a scruffy exterior he was obviously a kind and humane person with much wisdom and insight into the human condition. From my association with Ernest, I learned never to judge people by their appearance but to be patient and allow them to reveal themselves in their own time.

14.

During our trips to the West End of London, Ted told me about some of his experiences as a film extra. He explained that he had a Union Card and had to pay monthly dues. There were times when he said he paid out more than he earned. Nevertheless, upon his prompting, I went along to the Film Extra's Union and was interviewed by a man who asked me whether I was related to the celebrated film director Brian Desmond Hurst, who had directed among many other things, the movie *Scrooge*, starring Alastair Sim. I was tempted to say 'yes' to see what would happen, but decided to admit that I was an unknown with no important affiliations. I was glad I told the truth because the interviewer later revealed that he knew the other Brian Hurst personally. In any case I was accepted as a member of the Union.

Sometime later I telephoned the Film Casting Agency inquiring about 'extra' work. To my surprise I was informed that if I went to Walton-on-Thames film studio the very next morning, where the Robert Morley *Oscar Wilde* movie was in production, I could be employed for one day. Several students from the Guildhall School had already done 'extra' work in the rival movie, entitled *The Trials of Oscar Wilde*, which strangely enough was in production at the same time. That particular movie was a high budget, wide-screen presentation in colour, and starred Peter Finch and James Mason. Both studios were racing to complete their sensational, biographical creations first. The Robert Morley version was in black and white, and starred John Neville as Lord Alfred Douglas and was obviously a much lower budget production.

I arrived at Walton-on-Thames film studio early the next morning and the security guard directed me to the appropriate hangar-like building. There, an assistant producer informed me that I would be doing a street scene, walking with a young lady on my arm, through a thick, pea soup London fog. I was supplied with an appropriate costume, complete with top hat, and told to get changed. Some other men were also getting into various costumes for different productions. They were curious about where I was working, and when I mentioned the *Oscar Wilde* movie, there were knowing looks and smirks passed between them. One rugged looking Irishman commented that I had the right sort of looks for the film industry, but I should avoid the 'casting couch.' I was a little embarrassed by his frankness, as I was quite shy in those days. I knew what he was referring to, but it was not my belief at the time that anyone in a key position would find me at all attractive. Both Oscar Wilde movies were about the repercussions of homosexual behaviour during the 'naughty nineties' in Victorian England. I am certain that one day a scientific reason will be discovered for this anomaly, and in the meantime people should not be persecuted for something they obviously cannot help. No person deliberately chooses to be a homosexual and as such they should be treated with understanding. Who knows? Perhaps the condition is Nature's own way of controlling the population and as it occurs frequently in the animal kingdom, it is perhaps not as unnatural as some might think.

It was a fascinating experience working in a film studio for the first time. My female partner, an attractive fair-haired girl with pale features, had to wear a large hat adorned with feathers, and we were both kept waiting interminably while fog machines spewed out the swirling grey substance, to the detriment of our sensitive lungs and throats. I remember sitting on a wooden crate watching director Gregory Ratoff advise Robert Morley in the playing of a scene with a Cockney newspaper boy, in which the street-wise boy was obviously being propositioned. Between takes they were chatting and joking about the subject matter, while Ratoff was offering suggestions for spicing up the scene without changing the rating of the whole movie. As far as I know, that scene was never used in the final cut, and as my partner and I were seen walking down the street for about two seconds of screen time, I could understand why making a movie might end up being such an expensive business. The outcome of that day's work at Walton-on-Thames Studio was complete loss of my voice, an embarrassing condition that lasted for several days. I am sure that present day environmentalists would have something to say on the matter.

Later in the year I was able to put in another day's work at Pinewood Studios on a movie called

Invasion Quartet, starring Spike Milligan. I was taken with a group of young men to be fitted out as a German Nazi soldier. We were all issued with rifles, and then piled on a bus which took us deep into the pinewood forest, where a replica of a concentration camp had been set up, complete with tall, barbed wire fence, a sentry box and an imposing gate. I remember it was a beautiful sunny day and we spent much time lying in the long grass munching snacks and talking. The movie was a comedy about Spike Milligan and his team being sent behind enemy lines to blow up a large gun nicknamed 'Big Bertha'. I had to ride on the back of a truck with other soldiers and jump off the moving vehicle, for which I was paid an extra pound 'danger money'. Later, during a gas bomb scare, we were required to panic by the open gates, hurriedly pull on gas masks and make a great deal of commotion, while Spike Milligan took advantage of the pandemonium by cheerfully riding a bicycle out through the open gates to freedom. It was a frothy and not very important comedy, and when I saw it in the cinema a year later, by the magical use of smoked lenses, all the action took place in the middle of the night and I could hardly see the faces of anyone on the screen!

Later, through the Guildhall School, I had the opportunity of working for the BBC in their Producers' Training Programme, which took place both at Baker Street and in Lime Grove Studios, Shepherds Bush. Fortunately the producers were not too worried about our acting skills, but more about our ability to remember our positions on the floor for the sake of the trainee cameramen.

In one comic skit I played a soldier hiding inside the wooden horse of Troy! Looking back, I see it all as useful confidence-building experience. I had to learn to be more assertive and positive in order to survive. The Guildhall School taught me much about public speaking, which was to prove of immense value a little later in my life when I had to stand on the platforms of Spiritualist Churches and demonstrate before total strangers. How this all happened, I will relate in a subsequent chapter.

Above: My first acting role as Jaques in Shakespeare's "As You Like It" produced at Huntingdon Grammar School in 1956. I am dressed in black and third from right.

15.

Leaving Brixton, I moved to a better area in Herne Hill, and took a small ground floor bed-sitter in the house of a kind and protective landlady named Mrs. Brookes. She had a pink, smiling face, and took me under her wing, frequently sending food to my room via her young son, Roger. She had a daughter Marion who was also kind and friendly. I was not eating properly at that time as I had little spare money and was literally a 'starving student.' Mrs. Brookes and her family were obviously aware of my condition but showed real interest in me as a drama student. They all went to see me perform in a production of Noel Coward's *Peace in our Time,* which played at the Guildhall Theatre during the middle of July 1960. (Coward's play is based on the premise that the Germans succeeded in invading England in 1940). Audrey Cameron, a veteran of the BBC, produced the show and I played the part of Stevie Shattock, a young cockney boy in the London resistance movement, attempting to free the country from Nazi domination. There I was, again encountering Nazis. I couldn't get away from them!

One day Mrs. Brookes suggested that I might like to meet a close neighbour who had worked for a famous composer. When I learned the composer was Gustav Holst who wrote *The Planets*, portions of which we had often used in our student acting classes, I was ready to go. The neighbour went by the delightful name of Miss Twistleton. She graciously invited us into her quaint front sitting room where she had several framed pictures of Gustav Holst on display. She extracted from the bookcase various examples of Holst's original manuscripts and I was allowed to look at these, wishing privately that I had been a little better educated in music theory. Miss Twistleton offered us tea and biscuits and told us some anecdotes about her work with Gustav Holst. It was a memorable afternoon.

About this time I also began attending lectures at The College of Psychic Science (as it was then called) in Queensberry Place, South Kensington. This amazing building had private séance rooms containing blue curtained areas for physical mediums to demonstrate, as well as a large upstairs lecture hall that displayed interesting paintings of some of the pioneers of psychic research. The college also had an excellent library and regular lectures by such well-known figures as Lord Dowding, who had led the Battle of Britain against the Germans. He had become a convinced Spiritualist as had his wife Lady Dowding, who was involved in the 'Beauty without Cruelty' movement. She had received much publicity in her attempts to persuade wealthy ladies to wear synthetic furs instead of the real thing. Lieutenant Colonel Reginald Lester was another respected lecturer. I attended his talk on the R101 airship disaster, and learned how a famous medium, Mrs. Eileen Garrett, while in trance had brought through technical details supposedly from the dead Captain of the airship, explaining the reason for the crash. Among psychic researchers this is regarded as one of the most powerful cases in support of the survival hypothesis.

Another tall and imposing character at the College was Brigadier Firebrace, who was a well-known Spiritualist, astrologer and author. Once when I was questioning the friendly Brigadier about the various merits of the sidereal versus the tropical zodiac, he looked down at me, grinned and said "Anyway, whichever system I use, I still turn out to be a Leo!"

The College also had regular demonstrations of clairvoyance and clairaudience by top mediums. To counterbalance this, psychic researchers would lecture on fraud and deception, relating their various experiences with a few rogues and scallywags and educating us about the need for caution when evaluating such phenomena. Sceptical magicians and hypnotists were also allowed to present their points of view, and although I didn't always agree with them, I found their accounts of 'exposed' fraudulent mediums interesting and entertaining.

In an evening discussion group led by Mr. Simeon Edmunds, who was an author and expert on hypnotism, I met a short, round-faced lady from Grays Thurrock in Essex. Her name was April Day and she had just published a slim volume of verse entitled *Sunshine and Showers*. I immediately liked her. She was my kind of person: honest, kind and down-to-earth. She told me she was the only surviving member of her family, and she came to London to sit with famous physical mediums in order to make contact with her beloved parents. After Mr. Edmunds had closed the discussion group, I sat talking to this very sweet lady and suddenly found myself observing a curious cloud floating in the air above her head. Inside the cloud I saw the image of a man with distinct features and a bushy moustache. The image looked like the negative of a photograph, as clearly as I can remember, and the name 'Georgie' kept coming into my mind. I suddenly felt an overwhelming urge to describe this experience to April. She jumped excitedly forward in her chair, smiled broadly and exclaimed: "That's my father you're describing. I always called him Georgie."

This incident cemented our friendship and later, April persuaded me to take a service at Grays Thurrock Spiritualist Church in Essex. With knees knocking, and considerable doubt about my ability to give messages, I remember standing before a congregation of mostly senior citizens and being aware of certain faces seeming brighter than others. I would initiate a conversation with those particular people, informing them of what I was receiving, and was relieved and delighted to know that my information was accurate and understood.

April informed me of her outstanding séances with the London independent voice medium, John Lovette. She explained how John had sat several times a week in a dark closet in his home with a friend named Mrs. Baines. They were not there for any romantic purpose, but she had been present to help him develop his physical mediumship. To those who are puzzled by the need for darkness I can only explain it using the following analogy:

In a similar way that a photograph is developed in a dark room because of the sensitivity of the paper to light, so during a physical séance a substance known as 'ectoplasm' has to be developed by spirit doctors and chemists in darkness. The unseen operators use the bodily fluids and vitality of the medium in order to create moving rods of energy that can interact with physical objects in the darkened room. In the case of genuine voice mediums, the spirits are able to create replicas of the human speech organs that float in the air and are used to produce the many different types of voices that can be heard in the séance room. Such a phenomenon is referred to as 'independent voice' because the medium's own vocal chords are never used. Today, with the aid of special infra-red viewers (night vision goggles), psychic researchers have been able to sit in the dark and watch the 'ectoplasm' emerging from the mouth, nose or ears of the physical medium, and also to photograph with special cameras this rare and elusive substance. Through the kindness of my friend April Day, I was later to experience such phenomena with a Sussex medium. However, my very first physical phenomena séance was to take place back in my Home County of Huntingdonshire (as it was then) with none other than Mrs. Ann Copley, the tiny medium my Aunt Dorry had raved about some years earlier. That turned out to be a truly mind-altering experience.

Above: April Day who persuaded me to give my first public demonstration at Grays Thurrock in Essex. April had sat with a number of physical mediums in order to contact her deceased parents and she had had great success in doing so. She was a good friend and confidant.

16.

Agnes Townsend, who later became Ann Copley, was born in the village of Warboys, on September 28th, 1905. It is significant to comment that this tiny village which overlooks the East Anglian fens, found its way into the history books in 1593 when a John and Alice Samuel and their daughter Ann, residents of the village, were executed following a rigged trial at Huntingdon, for allegedly casting a spell upon Lady Cromwell of Hinchingbrooke Castle, causing her to die. Members of the Samuel family were dubbed 'the witches of Warboys' and their so-called crimes, based upon flimsy evidence, marked a period when anyone with some degree of second sight, or who refused to attend the Church of England on a regular basis, might be condemned as a witch, or sorcerer, in some cases on the whim of a malicious child. It is possible that with the name of 'Samuel', the family might also have had a Jewish background, adding a further reason for their persecution. Remember, that in those days it was mandatory to attend church on Sunday, whether you believed or not, and the local Lord of the Manor had considerable power in enforcing this, so by disobeying the rules you could easily fall foul of the local authority. There is little doubt in my mind that if Ann Copley had been born three hundred years earlier she might also have been persecuted and branded a 'witch.'

I know little of Ann's early life, but from some of her personal notebooks that were passed on to me by Mrs. Irene Speller of the firm of Copley's at St. Ives, I have discovered that Ann was able to fall into trances during her late twenties and was probably involved with Spiritualism even earlier than that. She had only a limited education and during the early 1930's she was employed as a domestic help at the home of Mr. H. Copley, senior. When it was known that Ann possessed strong mediumistic abilities, young Mr. Robert Copley who had lost his beloved fiancée, Peggy, in a tragic accident, eagerly sought the maid's services.

Soon, in the early 1930's, Ann was conducting very successful séances for her employers on a regular basis. She was controlled by an entity that claimed to be a little Red Indian girl named 'Chastan.' Chastan had a high-pitched childish voice and an infectious giggle. Nevertheless, this little guide speaking through Ann gave numerous and detailed descriptions of deceased people the medium had never known. Chastan was always extremely kind and cheerful, and often amazed the sitters with words of profound wisdom.

Eventually a romance blossomed between Ann and young Mr. Robert, who himself had cheated death a number of times by surviving against impossible odds horrendous motor cycle accidents and major damage to his back. His father had been converted to Spiritualism after the death of two children (one child had fallen down a well), and Robert was to follow in Dad's footsteps, becoming an inspirational speaker and a very powerful magnetic healer. It seemed predestined for Ann and

Robert to get together and they were married in 1939, the year after my birth. 'Bob' (as I later called him) towered over his diminutive wife, and as he had received a good education and was somewhat intellectual, he usually thought that he knew best. Ann, however, had a mind of her own, was intensely practical, good-natured to friends and family, and would sometimes poke fun at her analytical husband. As Bob was born on the early morning of September 3rd, 1902, with Leo rising and the sun in Virgo, he liked to be king of his own castle. Fortunately, Ann had the Moon, Mercury and Venus all in Virgo, so she was quite in tune with her unusual husband. In one way she kept him grounded, and in another way, through her powerful mediumship, she helped his spirit soar.

When these dear friends knew that I was taking an occasional Spiritualist meeting in the London area and doing a few private sittings at my home in North London, I was invited down to the country to their little bungalow called 'Waterways' in the village of Hemingford Grey. Nearby was a small lake with exotic birds and many naturalised wild flowers. In the back garden Bob and Ann had converted a large barn into a Sanctuary for their healing work and for the physical phenomena séances. Dorry had by this time fully recovered from the tuberculosis and had rejoined the Copley circle. Mrs. Mabel Hammond, the ex-headmistress of a local school and several other nice people were also in the group.

One thing that amused me about Ann was her declaration that she would be very frightened if she were to witness any of the phenomena produced through her own mediumship. Consequently she sat on a wooden chair surrounded by curtains and was always taken off into deep trance. The lights would be totally extinguished, and then through the magic of luminous paint we could all clearly see various objects on the floor or on a nearby table. Several aluminium trumpets would always be placed in the centre of the circle, together with a bowl of clean water. I understand the water was to assist the spirit chemists in the production of the necessary power, enabling levitation of the trumpets, ringing of bells and voices to eventually manifest in the air.

Ann quickly fell asleep, and after a few moments could be heard gently snoring behind the curtains. We commenced singing '*Jerusalem*' and '*Abide with Me*' to a previously recorded tape. Within a short time the luminous trumpets started jiggling on the floor. Two of them suddenly rose in the air and began circling over our heads at tremendous speed. I felt my heart begin to beat quickly. This was truly an amazing thing to witness. One of the trumpets dropped with a metallic clang to the floor while the other trumpet slowed down and began hovering slightly above us. Suddenly the voice of a London cockney man named Johnny began speaking through the trumpet. To my astonishment he addressed me, noting that I was new to the circle.

"Don't worry, mate, I won't come too near ya, if you're feeling windy," he reassured me. He was right. I was feeling a little nervous. To see luminous objects moving about at rapid speed in the dark, and then to hear an unexpected voice unlike anyone's in the room, can give you quite a jolt. I immediately thought about the possibility of accomplices hiding behind the scenes, or loud speakers being placed cleverly in the dark. Then, when other members of the circle spoke to Johnny and he showed knowledge of events that they had not shared with any of us, let alone the medium, I began to think again.

Soon Johnny communicated with my Aunt Dorry:

"Your brother's 'ere, gal. He wants to 'ave a few words wiv you and Brian."

"Oh tell him to go ahead!" Dorry said. She was desperately hoping to hear from her younger brother Frank, who had been killed in a motor cycle accident just after his twentieth birthday.

The trumpet continued to be levitated, there was a brief silence and then another male voice spoke, addressing Dorry and myself with terms of affection. He told Dorry that he was so relieved she was cured of the TB and that there was love and healing all around her. He said that he was there with his own mother, who had died of the same disease, and that he had lots of friends in the spirit world and was really enjoying himself over there. Then he spoke directly to me, rather taking me off guard by referring to a private and personal matter regarding a disappointment in my love life. He urged me to be patient, and then he said something that showed astonishing knowledge of recent events: "You know,

Brian, you mustn't go to school in London without any breakfast in your stomach. It's not good for you. I'm talking about every day last week."

He was quite right. I had always eaten a bowl of cereal in the morning or had a few slices of toast and marmalade, but for some reason I had not done that during the previous week, as I had been in a hurry to get to a class at my college. Frank promised to help me in my life and to send along certain people who would open doors for me to continue my work in the Spiritualist movement. I had a strong emotional reaction to this message and felt that this uncle I had never known, really cared.

During the course of the séance, a number of other people spoke through the trumpet, and each voice had its distinctive quality. I hardly heard what they were saying to the nearby sitters, as my mind was going over the wonderfully kind words of support I had just heard from my father's dead brother. I began to realise there was nothing to fear while sitting in a physical phenomenon circle. Truly God's angels were ministering unto us, and though knowledgeable of our weaknesses, the fact that they had walked this earth themselves, made them so much more able to understand the conflicts and problems facing us daily in the physical existence.

The voice and trumpet phenomena lasted for about twenty minutes. The final communicator commented that the power was dropping and that Chastan was waiting to speak through the medium. The trumpet then fell to the floor and in a short time the little-girl voice of the guide began addressing each one of us with words of homespun wisdom. She was extremely amusing, being quite as entertaining as any music hall act. When her cheerful optimistic voice addressed me she commented that my "uncle man" had a lot in common with me, but he was a lot bolder and that he was going to give me a push and help me with the confidence that I didn't have.

Looking back, this first séance with Ann Copley comforted me considerably and gave me a more philosophical outlook towards my life. I became less afraid of rejection, and decided that I must put all my efforts into making a success of life and realising some of my dreams.

17.

People often asked whether any of my experiences in Spiritualism have ever scared me. There is one that stands out in my memory. It happened while I was still a drama student and living in the Shepherds Bush area of London. Several of my friends from the Guildhall School had become deeply interested in holding séances. One of the girls had rented a room in Elsham Road, W.14, just a couple of streets away from me. I was invited there one evening as she and some other Guildhall students were having a party and later wanted my participation in a table-tipping session.

When I arrived I noticed that the alcohol was flowing freely, and I was vaguely troubled by that fact, but joined in the party spirit by having just one glass of wine. Also at the party was another boy from my hometown named Alex Williams and a Michael Lewin from the Guildhall, both of whom were probably quite sceptical. Among the girls present was a beautiful actress named Daphne, a lively dancer named Christine, and a couple of other girls I cannot remember. It was quite a small and enthusiastic group.

Later we lit a candle and placed it in the centre of the table, turned out the lights and sat around expectantly. Within a short time everyone could feel cold breezes. The window and door were both closed. I began to feel extremely uneasy. I felt chills down the back of my neck and had goose bumps on both forearms. Daphne commented that she was also feeling nervous.

Suddenly the candle went out. One minute it was burning brightly, the next we were in pitch darkness. No one was prepared for what happened next. A powerful, unseen force seemed to emanate from the centre of the table and Alex and Michael, who sat on opposite sides, were both pushed violently backwards from their seats, the unexpectedness of it causing them to cry out with fear. Someone yelled: "Turn on the light!"

As Daphne flipped the switch, the light came on and we were able to clearly see both boys lying on opposite ends of the carpet in a state of shock.

"What happened?" Michael groaned.

"Someone doesn't want us at the table," Alex commented.

No sooner had both boys got to their feet than the electric light also failed. Once again we were plunged in darkness.

"I don't like this!" I commented.

Christine managed to find the matches and once again lit the candle. One of the other girls was shivering uncontrollably. Going out on to the landing, we discovered that the whole house was in darkness and people were emerging from their rooms to enquire what had happened.

"I think the main fuse has gone," Michael said.

Someone found him a flashlight and to his credit he went downstairs and fixed the fuse. After that we rapidly found a Bible and opened it to the twenty-third psalm. We said a prayer and asked for a blessing on the spirits in the house. The cold chill rapidly disappeared, but the party of good friends broke up, chatting animatedly about the strange incidents around the table.

The whole point of this true story is to emphasise that séances should never be seen as party games. Nor should anyone take alcohol prior to a séance. Even slight inebriation apparently causes changes in the rate of vibration of the auric lights that surround us, producing disturbances in our own protective envelope of spiritual-electrical energy. These changes can be perceived by earthbound or less desirable entities that might well be attracted to them as a moth to a flame, the consequences of which could be a negative energy infiltration of the electromagnetic envelope of the unsuspecting individual. Very high sexual energy can also attract some entities, and a group of young men and women sitting in darkness around a table have plenty of that kind of energy.

There is no doubt that all of us on the spiritual path do need to watch our environment, our associates and our own thoughts and actions. It is quite possible for the policeman to become even more corrupted than the criminal he hunts, because of the dangers that may arise from his association with devious and unevolved energies. I can well understand why Jesus went into the wilderness to pray, and Indian yogis often live apart from the general community. Nowadays I find the atmosphere of large cities quite stifling, and am perfectly happy to spend many hours alone in my garden or to get lost in a good book!

During my early years serving Spiritualist churches in the London area I was amazed and appalled by the extreme jealousy and rivalry I encountered on numerous occasions. One famous platform clairvoyant wrote me an extremely rude letter because I had dared to give my telephone number to a lady at one of his meetings. This had been observed by one of the medium's entourage who had, no doubt, exaggerated the incident, and when reporting it, added fuel to the fire. At another church in Southeast London, the thin, elderly woman in charge began whispering information to me about members of the congregation during the singing of the hymn prior to the demonstration. I was so astounded by her apparent lack of faith in my ability to perform that I ignored everything she told me and came up with some good nitty-gritty evidence for people that she had not even mentioned. As a result, the 'resident medium' was rather aloof after the meeting and I was never invited to her First Spiritualist Church again. I was quite happy with that outcome.

I often attended Sunday meetings at The Spiritualist Association of Great Britain. In those days, 'Belgrave Square' as it was called, had a talented organist named Harold Pook, and several eminent pianists were often invited to play wonderful atmospheric music in the upstairs lecture hall before the meetings began.

There was also a lively restaurant in the basement where you could always meet someone friendly and interesting. In that very restaurant I met an elderly widowed man who showed me the most extraordinary photographs taken at a Helen Duncan materialisation séance. His dead wife had fully appeared to him, clothed in long, white ectoplasmic drapery. She had sat on his knee and he had been able to put his arm around her and speak with her on intimate matters for several minutes. The photographs had been taken, I understand, with special infrared film to avoid the harmful effects of a flash upon the tenuous ectoplasmic substance that made up the materialisation. With tears in his eyes, the elderly gentleman assured me that there was no doubt in his mind that the figure who seated herself upon his lap was indeed his beloved wife. The miracle to him was that she had manifested as a much younger woman, and looked very much the way he remembered her at the time of their wedding many years previously. The good news, it would seem, is that 'old age' is only a temporary inconvenience of the physical body!

At 'Belgrave Square' I was able to meet several of the really great mediums of the time. William Redmond was always particularly good when he came to me with a message. On one occasion he amazed me by speaking of a boy named Michael Marshall who had lost one eye in a game of bows and arrows. Michael had been in one of my classes at junior school, and his mother had also died not long after the accident. I remember as a child having been very upset over this, and feeling quite sorry for Michael. Mrs. Marshall was apparently the communicator, and she thanked me for my genuine sympathy and gave me a beautiful message through William Redmond.

On another occasion with Nora Blackwood, who was equally famous, the medium spoke of a school friend named Ken who had died of Leukaemia. This was perfectly true. I was asked to visit Ken's parents who lived near a railway station and to convey his message that he was not really dead and that he loved them.

When I next visited Huntingdon I had a vague recollection of where my deceased friend had once lived. I visited the row of small cottages in the evening and knocked on a door, hoping that someone could give me directions to the family I wanted. To my utter astonishment, it was Ken's father who opened the door. I can remember very little of the conversation I had with him and his wife, but I was invited in and given a cup of tea while I explained the extraordinary circumstances surrounding Nora Blackwood's message. Both parents stared at me in disbelief, but they were polite, and although I never saw them again, I can only hope that my words brought them some comfort and consolation in the sad loss of their teenage son. At least I had carried out Ken's wishes.

I changed my address in London a number of times during those early years. My mother complained that she had run out of pages in her address book, keeping track of me. At one point I was reunited with Geoffrey Keay and his Italian wife, Toni. I had a small bed-sitter next to their flat on the first floor of a Tufnell Park terraced house. Geoffrey's mother, Stella, who was now divorced, was also living in the room above mine. She was a cheerful lady who would sing loudly at the weekend, clump up and down the stairs and wake me up early on a Sunday! Another ex-Guildhall student named Peter Schofield, a long-time friend, also lived in the house. Peter was a tall, intensely kind boy with a somewhat nervous and dramatic personality. He was a Scorpio and obviously very psychic, and at times was able to clearly see spirits. On one occasion he gave me a very detailed message about a previous life I had had in Paris.

"There's an eighteenth century French nobleman here!" he exclaimed, staring into space, "I think he might be one of your spirit guides, Brian."

Peter had the unusual habit of raising his right arm and pushing the little finger of his hand into the outer corner of his right eyeball. I presumed that by distorting his vision he was able to get a better look at the spirit under observation. Some years later, at a Leslie Flint voice séance, Peter's messages to me were totally confirmed, and I will give details of how I actually spoke to this Frenchman in a subsequent chapter.

As nearly all the inhabitants of the house were believers in Spiritualism, we decided to form our own physical phenomena circle and to sit in Stella's top room once a week. During the sittings we always had a bowl of water on the floor of the séance room and a couple of luminous 'trumpets' standing nearby. We were sitting for the levitation of the trumpet and possibly the independent voice. We studied many Spiritualist handbooks on the subject and everyone was keen and supportive.

The group sat regularly for about two and a half years and at the end of that time we were showing definite signs of progress. Tiny lights began floating about in the room. The trumpets were sometimes moved across the carpet, though not yet lifted. We always placed them well out of reach of everyone's arms and legs, to avoid inadvertent kicking. On several occasions the trumpet was observed spinning and wobbling. I was always in deep trance at this time and when I returned to normal consciousness I would be aware of a strange sensation of pins and needles throughout my whole body. It was in this development circle that the spirit of an Indian yogi named Ramananda first entranced me. When he was in control, I was sometimes distantly aware of myself speaking words, but being unable to stop the flow or to interfere in any way with what was being said. Sometimes I would think that perhaps the yogi was a figment of my own brain, or some kind of split-off personality. However, Ramananda would frequently tell members of the circle about things I knew nothing of and surprisingly he actually predicted that I, (the medium) would one day visit India and reside there for a time. Such a possibility seemed highly unlikely, but Fate had a few surprises in store for me.

One day my friend Christine from the Guildhall School contacted me and wanted to bring some friends along to our weekly séance. Not realising that there could be an element of risk to my personal safety, I agreed to allow the extra visitors, after consulting the other members of our regular circle.

On the appointed evening we all gathered in the upstairs séance room. I sat in my usual canvas folding chair set back in a closet in the corner of the room and the lights were extinguished. Within a short time I began to drift into trance. The comforting darkness allowed me to relax totally. I would often experience the sensation of floating just above my body. Sometimes it felt as though the chair had dropped from beneath me and I was suspended in a warm and comforting atmosphere. I gradually lost all awareness of the room and the people sitting there expectantly.

Soon I was jerked unpleasantly back to reality by a woman's high-pitched scream. I heard Peter Schofield say "Look at the trumpet! It's moving!" One of the visiting girls said, "Open the door! I want to get out!"

She was obviously quite frightened by what she had seen. The very intense and physically painful sensations I experienced at that moment are still clearly remembered. I groaned out loud, feeling as though my whole solar plexus area was being pulled from my body. Something hot, that had a strange odour, appeared to be rushing back between my teeth. I can only say that it was somewhat analogous to 'reverse vomiting' if such impossibility can be imagined. The whole experience was extremely shocking to my physical body.

Geoffrey Keay quickly realised that I was suffering some injury. The lights were turned on and he was kind enough to help me out of the room. I felt weak and ill for several days and commented to my circle members that I did not want to be a physical medium. It was far too dangerous.

Of course the obvious mistake we all made was to allow new people into the séance room during a very critical phase of our development. The unsuspecting visitors were quite unprepared for the manifestations of spirit. They probably hoped for messages and not movement of objects. Looking back on this event, had it not been for the shock to my system and the genuine concern it engendered within me, I might today be one of the well-known physical phenomena mediums. As it happened, I rejected that line of development, but still became an internationally known mental medium. Fortunately that experience of being injured did not discourage me from sitting with others who were gifted with the rare and amazing ability to materialise the spirits, as I will relate in the following chapter.

18.

At this time, most of us were also attending the demonstrations of famous medium Joseph Benjamin, which were held at the Foresters' Hall, Kentish Town, just a short trip south on the Underground. Joe Benjamin was amazing for his uncanny ability to transmit complete names and addresses of deceased people with relevant information to identify them. Joe was the son of an East London Jewish tailor and he had discovered his gift at an early age. Geoffrey Keay was invited to sing from the platform on several occasions and I was also asked to give short talks and the invocation prior to Joe's demonstration, which would last for about an hour.

Joe was a brilliant medium. He was a little, thin Capricorn man with round shoulders, a restless fidgety body, bullet-shaped head and horn-rimmed glasses. His messages were always somewhat down-to-earth, direct, and delivered with an air of omniscience. He believed that he was one of God's prophets and should be respected accordingly. When a woman in the audience dared to refer to him as "Joe" he immediately corrected her and insisted upon being called "Mr. Benjamin." He had a very patient, longsuffering wife named Kitty who sat at the back of the hall and collected the money. There were times when he made unkind remarks to her, and these incidents made me somewhat wary of him, as he was known to be quite jealous and had a sharp tongue.

Through my regular attendance at Joe's meetings I became friendly with his pianist, an extremely sweet and gentle lady named Lillian Bolsch. There was something of a previous century about her. She used muslin and lace in her unusual dresses and she would come on stage in an assortment of rainbow colours that gave her a somewhat 'fairy-like' appearance. She was an excellent pianist and definitely brought 'good vibrations' to the meetings. She had an extremely kind and compassionate face and rather sleepy eyelids as she turned and smiled at the audience.

What an audience it was, too! The hall was always packed and the messages were extremely dramatic in their delivery. Joe knew how to play upon the emotions of the crowd, and although many of the audience were working class people with little education, there was no doubt that they took their Spiritualism seriously and Joe was their hero.

I will always remember and love Lillian. She was the first one to warn me about Joe's jealousy. She later helped me in a number of ways and I became a frequent visitor to her little bungalow in Northolt, Middlesex, where she took care of her husband Billy and ten cats. The house was always clean and free of odours and Lillian herself was a delightful hostess. Lillian's daughter, Cynthia Pearl, was a talented dancer and performed all over Europe, being thrown in the air and magically caught by the men in her troupe. Strangely enough the whole family was born under Pisces! I later discovered that Lillian had some remarkable healing powers, and I was to experience some strange events through my friendship with this highly spiritual and completely unworldly lady.

After one of Joe's meetings she called me aside and asked whether I would like to attend a physical phenomena séance with the well-known medium William Olsen. I had heard about this extraordinary man many times through lectures and discussions I had attended at the College of Psychic Science. Some of the researchers there utterly refused to believe in Olsen's authenticity, stating that he was an expert escape artist like Houdini, and in some clever way could release himself from the ropes which always bound him to a solid oak chair during the sittings. Of course I accepted Lillian's invitation, and as Peter Schofield was accompanying me at the time, he was also included.

The following week we duly arrived at the terraced house in Messina Avenue, Kilburn, and met our kind hostess, Mrs. Anna Corbett. We were ushered into a large Victorian front sitting room with a high ceiling and about twenty-five chairs set out in a circle. Lillian arrived soon afterwards, with the rest of the people, and eventually Mr. and Mrs. Olsen emerged from Anna's back room. Peter and I approached Mr. Olsen and introduced ourselves. Mrs. Olsen suggested that we might like to be the ones who searched her husband prior to the sitting, and we agreed to do this.

As the sitters were being seated alternately male/female in the large room, Peter and I carefully searched this genial, elderly man who was the subject of so much controversy. He dropped his trousers in the back room and even let us look inside his underwear to demonstrate that he was not concealing anything that could be used in the darkened room to deceive or aid in his escape from the ropes that were to bind him. We were perfectly satisfied that the man was truthful and concealing nothing but his naked flesh.

Mr. Olsen entered the séance room in a striped shirt and a pair of dark pants. I requested that I might sit next to him during the proceedings and he willingly agreed to this. When he was seated in a solid wooden armchair, he was given a rather tattered tweed jacket to wear. Once this was on, a lady with a needle and thread kneeled down in front of him and actually began to stitch the jacket together. It then became clear that even though he might undo the buttons, he would not be able to separate the two parts or easily free himself from the jacket. I watched this procedure with fascination, wondering what would be the outcome.

When the lady had finished, two men brought strong ropes and Mr. Olsen had his hands bound to the arms of the chair, his chest bound to the back of the chair and his legs bound to the bottom rails of the chair. Finally, a dimmer knob that was attached to an electric cable was fastened to the left arm of the chair (on my side). I observed that although Mr. Olsen was secured firmly, he could still operate the knob to brighten or dim a red light that was in the middle of the circle on a stand. In front of the medium were placed on end two luminous trumpets. On a small table in front of me lay a luminous tambourine and a drum and drumsticks. There were also some small bells coated with luminous paint.

Finally, each one of the sitters was linked together at the wrist with a thick rubber band, so that if anyone left their chair in the dark, their neighbours would immediately know it. Considering the unlikely possibility that three people in the group were in collusion with the medium, so that the centre one of the three could break the circle and fraudulently create phenomena, the controls seemed adequate at that time. I was banded to a ginger-haired lady on my left, and the medium was to my right and slightly in front of me. My right hand was not bound and I could easily reach out and touch him if I wished.

One of the men locked the séance room door, putting the key in his pocket. He then took his seat, and slid his hands through the rubber bands of his neighbours. Mrs. Olsen, who was sitting opposite me on the other side of her husband, turned out the lights and we could all see the luminous objects glowing brightly in the dark.

An opening prayer was said, and then some tape-recorded music was played and we were all asked to sing 'Abide with me'. Mrs. Olsen led the singing in a not-very-tuneful voice. Later the tone of the music changed to a livelier beat as we sang "The Yellow Rose of Texas' and 'She'll be coming Round the Mountain'. During the singing of the latter numbers, both trumpets jiggled and suddenly rose in the pitch-blackness. We saw the luminous bands around them streak by as the trumpets flew into the furthest corners of the room, tapped on the ceiling

143

above us and a moment later cheekily descended to float horizontally in front of us as they slowly moved around the circle. I could hear the somewhat laboured breathing of the medium followed by the voice of a North American Indian guide who greeted us all, assuring us that the power was very good, and for the next two and a half hours the séance proceeded with gusto!

Unfortunately I was not able to tape record the meeting, but it turned out to be one of the most spectacular séances I have ever witnessed. The spirits appeared to be on top form and roughly speaking the séance was divided into two parts: The first one-and-three-quarter hours were conducted in complete darkness. Not only did numerous voices come and speak through the trumpets, but also the communicators were frequently recognised by the sitters because of personal details that were mentioned. At one point a trumpet approached the ginger-haired lady to my left and the voice of a woman spoke to her. 'Ginger' recognised it as her dead mother by the names and information given. She became rather upset and I heard the spirit voice say "Darling, I was so sorry you didn't get my ring. You know it was stolen from my body in the hospital mortuary."

"Oh mother, now I know it's really you!" Ginger replied with deep emotion. After the séance she told me that no one in that room could have known about the things her mother mentioned.

Soon a little spirit girl named 'Topsy' came to liven up the proceedings. The trumpet hovered in front of me and a childish voice said: "I like you. I'd like to come and sit on your lap!"

Being young and still rather nervous I didn't encourage her to do that. Instead, I asked her a question: "Topsy, how do we appear to you? Do we look transparent?"

She giggled delightedly: "All I can say is you've got a nice clean shirt on and clean underwear!"

I was somewhat taken aback by this flippant reply. She lost interest in me immediately and the trumpet flew over to a man sitting opposite me in the circle.

"I like you too," she said, "You've got nice legs! Can I give you a big kiss?"

"All right," he said agreeably.

The next moment we all heard the sound of a loud kiss in the dark.

"That was a wet one, Topsy!" the man commented, "I felt it right on my cheek."

"You're nice!" she added saucily, as the trumpet flew over to someone else. Topsy continued with her amusing patter for quite a few minutes. I had heard that she could embarrass sitters from time to time by her childlike directness. She obviously liked good-looking men and was somewhat precocious for a little girl.

Soon a small boy's voice could be heard through the trumpet: "Shall I play my drum for you?" he asked.

"Yes, please!" the sitters chorused.

I sat completely spellbound as the luminous drum and drumsticks levitated in the darkness around us, and the unseen child began to beat out a catchy

145

rhythm in what sounded like a very professional manner. Both drum and drumsticks floated around the circle so that everyone could see this amazing thing.

Then the tambourine and bells levitated and for some minutes there was quite a commotion as all the instruments played together. Anyone passing by in the street outside would have thought that a noisy party was in progress.

Later, speaking through the entranced medium, the American Indian guide told us that we had a distinguished visitor, who wished to sing to us. Who could it be?

It turned out to be the famous music hall entertainer, Mr. Harry Lauder. One of the trumpets rose high in the air and through it came this most beautiful baritone voice singing a religious song, which I had not heard before. Regrettably I cannot remember the title, but I heard someone in the room say quickly that it was a Negro spiritual. After the séance I spoke with one man who had a large collection of Harry Lauder 78 r.p.m. records.

"That was so incredible," the man said, "Harry Lauder never recorded that song, and I have every one of his records."

How astonishing that a Harry Lauder fan should have been privileged to hear in that very room the post mortem voice of the maestro himself! It certainly makes you think!

During the latter part of the séance, the guide announced that the red light would be turned on. He said that it was time for us to see the 'ectoplasm' that had made the phenomena possible. I was literally bursting with curiosity and leaned forward in my chair as the darkness dissolved into a pink brilliance. I was able to see everyone seated around the room and noticed that the entranced medium's left hand (closest to me) was turning the knob that had been fixed to the arm of the chair, in order to bring up the light.

Next, there was a strange gurgling noise from the medium's throat, and as I stared at his mouth I noticed a broad band of silk-like material slowly emerge from his lips. His mouth was slightly open and his head slumped forward on his chest. At first it looked like a handkerchief emerging as some kind of weave appeared on it, but as it descended lower and lower, creeping over his trousers like a long, flowing ribbon, I saw it touch the carpet and begin to move slowly out into the middle of the room. It looked pink because of the nearby light, but I guess its natural colour would be a greyish-white.

Meanwhile the guide was giving us a commentary from the same lips: "This is ectoplasm! This is what we make people from! Today not enough to make complete person. We show you arm and hand!"

And sure enough, the end of the ectoplasm rose in the air and appeared to be moulded into a perfectly formed arm and hand. The hand opened and closed its fingers. I could clearly see the nails shining. The arm rotated and then the materialisation seemed to melt away and the ectoplasm began to move back towards the medium. It slowly moved up his jacket, over the top of the ropes and once again disappeared inside his mouth. He appeared to gulp it down. I was close enough to see everything in detail, and I know that I was not hypnotised or hallucinating. I questioned other sitters at the end of the séance. They all reported seeing the same thing. But this was only a prelude to further spectacular events.

"We are now going to remove the medium's jacket," the guide announced.

As I stared curiously at the entranced man I saw the fingers of his left hand begin to dim the red light. At the same time his jacket appeared to be rippling and moving. There was a slight mist appearing around his body. The light was dimmer now but I could still clearly see William Olsen. Very quickly the jacket appeared to pass right through his body. Then an invisible force flipped the jacket on to the floor at my feet, making me retract my legs nervously.

"Now we will levitate the medium," the guide's booming voice continued.

We all watched, frozen with astonishment, as the wooden armchair began to rise towards the ceiling. The light became dimmer and I could barely see the chair floating above us. After a moment we heard the voice of the guide speaking from above and from a different location in the room.

"Keep in your feet! We bring medium down!"

There was a quick shuffling sound as people tucked their feet under their chairs. We heard a loud thump on the floorboards and the guide's voice, now speaking from our level, said: "That is all for tonight. God bless you! In a moment you may turn on your white light."

When Mrs. Olsen switched on the light we were surprised to see the medium still roped to his chair, but sitting in a completely different part of the room. He groaned, came out of his trance and looking around in a rather dazed manner said: "Oh, I see you've had results!"

It was the biggest understatement of the evening. We had had *magnificent* results! After a moment I picked up the jacket that lay at my feet and examined it carefully. It was still buttoned and the thread that had stitched it together was unbroken. The spirits had done the physically impossible. They had passed physical matter through physical matter. Apart from the previous sitting with Ann Copley, I had never seen such positive proof of the reality of a spiritual realm. It was at that time one of the most outstanding Spiritualist events I had ever witnessed. Later, I was to experience more personal contacts that would move me to tears.

Alex Williams took this photo of me by the sphinx on the embankment of the River Thames in London. Alex was from my home town and was a student at St. Martins School of Art. He later became a famous landscape painter of the Welsh borderlands.

19.

Shortly after the amazing William Olsen séance, my friend April Day spoke to me of an excellent physical medium who lived on the south coast of England at a place called West Worthing.

April invited me to meet her at the hotel where she would be staying prior to the séance. She was allowed to take one visitor along, and it was my good fortune to be accompanying her.

On the appointed spring day I was blessed with good weather. I took the train down to Brighton, caught a bus to West Worthing and quickly found April's hotel. I arrived around 4 p.m. to the announcement that as it was such a beautiful afternoon we were to be served tea in the garden. Birds sang loudly in the trees as the waitress left us with our tray of tea, sandwiches and cream cakes.

April had already seated herself at the round, white table and I grabbed a canvas deck chair to join her. As I seated myself, there was a loud unexpected noise of ripping material. The seat of the chair suddenly split beneath me and I fell heavily on my bottom and backward on to the grass, my feet raised in the air. We both began to laugh heartily. Picking myself up I managed to find a safe seat, while the tears ran down April's face.

"Oh, that was so funny!" she giggled, "I hope you're not hurt."

I knew her well enough not to be embarrassed.

"No bones broken," I said.

We finished our tea while April told me of some of the amazing results she had obtained on previous occasions with the medium whose circle we were attending that very evening. His name was Jim Hutchings and again he had a North American Indian guide named 'Moonstone.'

Jim and Betty Hutchings had a pleasant semi-detached house in Hailsham Road. That evening we arrived fifteen minutes before the séance was due to begin. Betty Hutchings, a round-faced, pleasant lady greeted us at the door and ushered us into a panelled front sitting room set out with chairs for about twelve people. In the blacked-out bay window area was a comfortable easy chair for the medium. A few sitters had arrived. One lady had come with her husband all the way from the north of England, hoping to speak to her dead son. I found myself hoping sincerely that she would be successful. To travel so far must mean that she had great faith in the medium's ability to obtain results. April and I took our seats near the back wall of the sitting room, close to an electric record player and a collection of old 78 records.

Soon the room was full of people. Betty Hutchings joined us, followed by her husband Jim, a thin, quiet man wearing glasses. Betty closed the door and locked it, and when all were seated, the lamps were turned off, allowing us to see the luminous glow of two trumpets standing on end near the medium's chair.

Betty opened with a prayer for protection and we all said The Lord's Prayer. Then the record player was started. We sang a couple of Christian hymns and these were followed by some livelier dance music. As the beat quickened, we saw the two trumpets lifted in the air, circling one another in a kind of spiral. So smooth were the movements, and so unusual in themselves that I instinctively knew there could be no ham-handed physical fingers attached to those trumpets.

Soon 'Moonstone' spoke through the medium while the luminous trumpets continued to entertain us with their rapid movement, spiralling and somersaulting and occasionally descending to tap one of the sitters gently on the back of a hand. It was quite fun to watch!

Soon a number of spirit voices began speaking to us through the trumpets. The couple from the north of England became very emotional when their dead son, killed in a car accident, began speaking about their overnight stay at a London hotel.

"Dad," the voice whispered through the floating trumpet, "I was there at the hotel with you. I saw you in the bathroom when you couldn't find your shaving cream. I tried to tell you which bag it was in. Then mum found it for you."

"That's quite true!" the father admitted.

His wife began to cry.

"I knew you were there!" she said.

"I love you, mum," the spirit voice whispered.

"We love you, too," his mother replied.

"I'm still interested in cars," the boy went on, "Of course I don't need one here. I only have to think about it and I can move from one place to another. It's real easy!"

"That's good," the mother responded more cheerfully.

They discussed personal family matters for a few more minutes and the 'dead' boy correctly named other relatives on earth who were not present at the séance. Afterwards, the couple told me that they had no doubt whatsoever that the voice was that of their beloved son who had died in his early twenties, a couple of years previously.

The séance continued and April was delighted when her father Georgie Whent-Day began speaking. The trumpet approached closer to us than I had ever seen it before. It was almost in April's lap.

"Good evening, young man!" he said to me, suddenly. And the trumpet moved between us. Before I could respond, he startled both of us by a pointed reference to the earlier event in the hotel garden.

"I was there when the chair collapsed," he said, "I saw it all! I hope you didn't hurt yourself."

Neither of us had mentioned this incident to anyone. This was supreme evidence that we had been under observation by the spirit world. The Hutchings had no idea which hotel April had been staying at. We both began laughing again as April's father continued speaking to her.

"When I saw those cream cakes, they really made my mouth water. Let me tell you also: when you threw those breadcrumbs to the birds, a bird over here was fed."

What an extraordinary idea, I thought.

Georgie spoke briefly of April's mother who was with him in the spirit world. She found it more difficult to speak through the trumpet.

"It takes a certain amount of *force*," Georgie explained.

As I stared at this luminous trumpet floating in the blackness in front of us, it suddenly reversed itself and the narrow end gently tapped April in her outstretched palm.

"You read my mind, Georgie," she said quickly.

The trumpet turned itself around again and Georgie gave us his love and departed. April told me afterwards that she had sent him a mental request to let her feel the narrow end of the trumpet, so that she would know definitely that the medium was not just holding it and speaking. Her unspoken request was granted. I thought that was rather a simple but smart test of the authenticity of the communication.

Another remarkable aspect of a Hutchings séance was the way in which beloved pets would sometimes make their appearance. One lady was told that her little budgerigar had not forgotten her and he was right there in the room. To my astonishment I heard the clear fluttering of wings and felt a sharp breeze pass my face as the spirit bird, apparently materialised, winged its way around the séance room. There were "Ooo's and "Ahhh's" as all the sitters experienced this feathered contact. Shortly afterwards we heard the yelping of a small dog that someone in the room recognised with deep emotion. 'Moonstone' assured us that all animals survived death, and those who had been close to loving humans, had been accelerated in their progress towards a higher life form. What a comforting idea! It somewhat agreed with the view held by devout Hindus. I had no doubt that there was gradual evolution on the life spiral and also reincarnation for some people, but exactly how it all operated was still a major mystery.

As no members of my own family came to speak to me at this séance, I arranged another sitting with Jim Hutchings several months later. This time I was unaccompanied and had a little more time to speak to Betty Hutchings before the séance began. I found Betty to be a very friendly and loving person. She said that she and her husband were both born in the sign of Gemini and each had been married before. They had ultimately met each other through the Spiritualist Movement and were very happy together. Betty took an immediate liking to me and said that I was welcome to join them at any of their meetings in the future. My only problem was that I lived and worked in London.

The séance began and soon different voices began speaking through the trumpets as they circled the darkened room. Some communicators were easily recognised by the sitters; others were not easily placed. At one point a deep voice speaking with a heavy European accent said he was the painter known on earth as Goya. He commented that the political problems of his time in the physical body had weighed greatly upon his spirit. Finally he had found peace in Heaven painting to the glory of God. I recollected that one of Goya's most famous earthly paintings dealt with *The Executions of the Third of May,* showing a French firing squad at work by lantern light, shooting ordinary men and women who are standing fearfully against a wall. Goya also painted a scene in a madhouse, as well as a number of other disturbing images. It had never occurred to me that such a famous man might attempt to communicate, and I was quite in awe at hearing the deep and resonant voice.

After some time the trumpet flew over to me and a spirit giving a Chinese name informed me that I was "a velly serious young man," and that I needed "more fun – yes?" He offered to bring me warmth of companionship. Laughingly, I thanked him. He departed and after some minutes I heard a female voice calling my name through the trumpet.

"Brian, can you hear me? It's Mary!"

"Is that Auntie Mary?" I queried.

"Yes, it is."

She was my grandfather's lovely second wife who had died of cancer while I was still at school. I remembered her snow-white hair and kind brown eyes and her particular way of speaking with a local St. Ives accent.

"I have a lovely house over here," she continued, "I'm really in Heaven. You should see my flowers in the garden. The hollyhocks are even taller than the ones we had at the bungalow."

I became quite emotional at this point, as I knew it really *was* her speaking to me. She had been a great gardener, and my grandfather always grew hollyhocks at the front of his bungalow. As a child I had often picked the flat disc-shaped seed pods or stuck my nose in the big velvety flowers.

"Are you happy now?" I asked.

"Of course I am, darling. It's never cold here and I'm young again. Some of the gardens here are tended by Jesus himself."

"It must be beautiful," I commented.

"Help people on earth," she whispered, "Tell people this truth," and the voice faded away.

It was the first time I had cried at a séance. I found the whole message particularly touching, as Auntie Mary had often taken care of me as a small boy, and her patience and sweet voice were forever in my memory. The possibility of Jesus working as a gardener in the great beyond was something I had not heard of before, and whatever we may think of such a concept Auntie Mary was over there and I was not. I had to take her words at face value.

My belief in the total authenticity of these communications was also reinforced when I heard Betty Hutchings requesting one of the spirit guides to intervene with help and healing for a local family who were experiencing apparently undeserved poverty and hardship. The guide promised that he would look into it and bring some good influence to the suffering people. To those that say these spirits are all demons in disguise and that "séances are the work of the devil," all I can say is that the 'devil' appears to be doing a great deal of good.

Above: Grandfather Arthur John Hurst with "Auntie Mary"

20.

Many people have told me over the years that they are totally bewildered by my ability to hear the voices and thoughts of those who have died. This gift did not come easily! In the early days of my development I went through a great deal of emotional pain. I am not whining or complaining about this. Apparently it had to occur in order to sensitise me and prepare me for the work that I was given to do. It would seem that whatever great gift may be bestowed upon us, there is also some kind of penalty to pay.

At one time the constant whisperings in my mind made me think I might be mildly schizophrenic. My sleep would often be disturbed at night by various entities trying to speak to me, and I would feel nervous fluttering in the region of my solar plexus. I would usually tell the entities to go away and leave me alone, and after some time my mind would quieten and I would eventually sleep.

This was a period of horrible sensitivity, and openness to suggestion. I experienced a great deal of sexual fantasising and picked up on the sexual energy of people standing next to me on the Underground train. I also felt the dark rage and pain of many people walking the city streets. I felt like a sponge, absorbing all the dross that floated in the air around me. I began to feel contaminated and unclean.

I have the theory that many spirit beings on the lower astral are very fascinated by our sexual energy and sometimes become voyeurs in our own private imaginings. I am sure that weak-minded people can also be influenced by some of these earthbound entities in a detrimental way. One needs to develop a strong sense of morality and ethics and to stay away from unpleasant places and people, who might by their low level of thought, attract such entities.

In order to strengthen my nervous system I began taking supplementary B vitamins and multi-minerals, as the thought had occurred to me that my openness to this sort of 'invasion' might be caused by nutritional deficiencies. I was, after all, primarily a vegetarian, although I could not bring myself to totally renounce the eating of fish, and being a young man living alone in London I was not always eating the healthiest of food. As I began taking the supplements, so the horrible sensitivity diminished.

If you, the reader, should find yourself experiencing some of the things I have just mentioned, it is a good idea to pay attention to possible nutritional deficiencies. Brewer's yeast is a powerful brain food and supplier of amino acids and B vitamins essential for good mental functioning. A large tablespoon of this should be dissolved in a glass of fruit juice every morning and taken prior to eating breakfast. I would not recommend this at night, as it might make you much too alert to sleep, but to wake you up and give energy in the morning it has few equals. My spirit guide, Dr. Grant, made me aware of the tremendous benefits of brewer's yeast as well as various other things. I thought it opportune to mention this, as others may be troubled in a similar way and need some suggestions for dealing with this problem.

One incident of an unexpected visitation that was indelibly engraved upon my memory occurred back in the early 1960's when I was still living in the Tufnell Park area of London. It was a foggy November evening and I felt a sudden urge to go and eat spaghetti at a small Italian restaurant in the nearby Holloway Road. It was already dark when I arrived on foot, and I was apparently only just in time to get a meal before the place closed. Half the chairs had already been stacked up on round tables in one part of the room. I was ushered to a small table in one corner and the waitress took my order.

While I was waiting for my food I noticed a solitary woman in a dark fur coat sitting at the next table. She appeared to be deep in thought and barely touching her dinner. I felt an oppressive atmosphere of deep gloom around her. Eventually my spaghetti arrived and I discovered after the waitress had left, that there was no Parmesan cheese on my table. The lady had a large container of it beside her, and I asked whether she would mind passing it to me. She appeared to resent my intrusion upon her thoughts, and rather abruptly handed me the grated cheese. It was just then that the most extraordinary thing began happening. As I was holding the bottle she had just given me, I became aware of whispering voices in my mind. The words and sentences were broken, like short telegrams of information:

"Boy in hospital...damage to head...talk to her...talk to her..."

Talk about what? I couldn't just turn to a total stranger in a restaurant and say that I was hearing voices. She'd think I was nuts! It might even scare her. Worst of all, supposing she didn't understand a word of it, I could look very foolish. I really must be imagining things I thought, and I continued eating my spaghetti. But the voices would not go away. A new sinister element came into the scenario running through my head:

"Suicide...she's got pills...she'll do it...stop her...talk to her now..."

This was too much for me. I became very uneasy and had absolutely lost my appetite for the delicious food in front of me. Suddenly I put down my spoon and fork and stared across at the woman in the fur coat. She did seem extremely unhappy. The darkness and distress around her seemed almost palpable. I was hesitating whether to speak when she suddenly looked up and stared back at me. There was no retreat.

"Excuse me," I ventured, tentatively, "But I am having some very strange thoughts right now and I have to speak to you about them."

She raised her eyebrows. I noticed she had dark circles under her brown eyes. I plunged in directly:

"Are you very worried about a boy in hospital with something wrong with his head?"

She in turn dropped her fork with a loud clatter.

"Oh my God! Is there any hope?"

"I don't understand this," I replied, "but a voice out of nowhere told me to talk to you."

"Please come and sit at my table," she requested.

I took my plate and sat opposite her. She looked up at me with tears in her eyes.

"That's amazing how you picked that up!" she said.

"Whatever it is that's troubling you," I continued, "is it so terrible that you've thought of ending your life?"

She fumbled with her bag on the edge of the table and removed a handkerchief.

"Yes, I was seriously thinking of doing it tonight."

"Why?"

"Oh, it's a long, sad story," she said, wearily.

"I'm willing to listen," I replied.

"I've just come from the hospital," she began, "I've been to visit my little son. He's eight, and mentally retarded."

"I'm sorry to hear that."

"Oh, I'm the one that should be sorry. It's my fault. It's all my fault!"

"How come?"

"Well, you see, when he was a baby, I dropped him on his head. He's been brain-damaged ever since."

"Now I understand," I said quietly, "But taking your own life isn't going to help this little boy who needs a mother."

"But I should be punished for what I did."

"Haven't you been punished enough already?"

"I don't think so."

I found myself staring at her handbag on the table.

"You know, you really must flush those pills down the toilet," I found myself saying, "They're right there in the bottom of your bag."

164

She looked startled: "How did you know that?"

"I'm a Spiritualist medium," I explained, "And sometimes dead people talk to me and tell me things. The voices in my head kept saying 'You must speak to her. You must stop her from doing that. It isn't the answer.'"

"Do you really think so?" she asked, wide-eyed.

"Why would I step into this place at this time and have these thoughts?" I counter-questioned, "It must be that God doesn't want you to do this terrible thing to yourself."

She stared at me again, crushing the handkerchief she was holding, "You must be right," she acknowledged, "But I still feel awfully guilty. I did such a terrible thing to my little son."

"But it was an accident that could have happened to anyone," I reassured her, "Small babies can be very slippery little creatures."

"Yes, he was wet from his bath when I dropped him," she related, in amazement, "He really did slip out of my hands, and as I was having severe back pain at the time I just wasn't fast enough to catch him."

"You see, it *was* an accident," I emphasised.

"But it's ruined his whole life," she whispered sadly.

"You mustn't give up hope," I continued, "He's all you've got!"

"That's true," she replied, "My husband left me for another woman just a year ago. He couldn't live with the pain I was going through. He never wanted to visit his son. He wanted us to forget we'd ever had a son. But I couldn't abandon my child."

"But that's what you would be doing if you took those pills and then turned on the gas oven."

"My God you're uncanny!" she said, screwing up her face, "That's exactly what I planned to do. How did you know that?"

"As I told you before, kind and well-meaning spirits must have sent me here to help you. Suicide isn't the answer. You could be lost in the levels of the lower astral, wandering about in the dark, constantly feeling that you'd been a total failure. That could be real Hell for you. You have to do something positive with your life. Help other people. Join a support group. Why don't you try writing a letter to the wonderful spiritual healer, Harry Edwards? He has a healing sanctuary at Burrows Lea in Shere, Surrey. They could put your son on an absent healing list. That man has actually performed miracles in front of the TV cameras."

"That's funny! I heard about Harry Edwards from someone else just a few weeks ago."

"Then listen to me. I know if it was my son, I'd want to try anything that might help."

"So you think there really is hope?"

"I do, and your son needs you to go on visiting him and taking him out. As he gets older, this condition could well improve. Haven't you thought of that?"

She smiled for the first time.

"You're very persuasive," she commented, "I begin to feel a bit better."

"Life takes a lot of courage, sometimes," I said, "But you must keep on fighting. It's the only way."

I remember patiently writing out the address of Harry Edwards' Healing Sanctuary on a scrap of paper. I also gave the lady my telephone number and asked her to let me know the outcome of any possible visit to the Sanctuary. I made her promise me that she would not take her own life. She thanked me for my help and said she realised that suicide was not the way to go.

Eventually we finished our meal and I escorted her to the bus stop. It was by now drizzling with rain. My last memory of her was watching her wave from the window of the departing bus, no doubt bewildered by the way in which a sensitive young man had been able to pick up her innermost thoughts and guide her in the right direction.

It would be very tempting to write a beautiful ending to this story, but the truth is, I never heard anything further from this woman. I don't know her name. I don't know whether she lived, or whether her son recovered. I can only hope that my presence in that restaurant, on that dark and drizzly night, served its purpose in some divine way and prevented a tragic event that could never have been undone. When you are a messenger, it would appear that your main task is to give the message in a non-judgemental way, hoping that reason and a sense of survival will, in the end, prevail.

21.

In previous chapters of this book I have described in some detail my early experiences, and a few of the people I met in my quest to develop my mediumship. I now jump forward to the year 1967. I had long left Tufnell Park and was at that time renting rooms in the home of a Bengali Indian artist in the Forest Gate area of London. He had limited English skills and so I frequently wrote his letters, aiding him in the marketing of his textile designs.

For several years I had been working for The Law Society. I had my own office and Dictaphone and would assist the Area Secretary, Miss Spicer in dealing with the Minutes of the legal aid meetings. I had to sign a secrecy paper as I was dealing with highly confidential material. In my role as clerical officer I dealt with divorce and damages for personal injuries. People applied for legal aid and it was part of my job to send notices to them regarding the acceptance or rejection of their applications for Civil Aid Certificates. I liked my job but after three years I felt the need for a change.

I applied to the London Borough of Waltham Forest for a possible position as a schoolteacher. At that time there was a great shortage of teachers and so I was gladly accepted on condition that I would attend training college and become qualified after a probationary year.

My experimental year of teaching had apparently been quite successful and before I began my studies at the North-Western Polytechnic in Kentish Town, my friend and landlord, whom I called 'Joe', suggested that I might like to accompany him and another Indian family to Bombay for a sightseeing trip. We would then travel by train across India, taking in New Delhi and then his hometown of Calcutta. It all sounded quite exciting!

I immediately remembered the words of Ramananda, the Indian yogi control, who had predicted some years earlier that I would visit his country. Prior to leaving for India I had a private sitting with a well-known Belgrave Square medium named Kathleen St. George. During the sitting, Kathleen St. George surprised me by giving me a serious health warning regarding my coming trip to Asia.

Joe, his friend Mrs. Saha and her two children had decided to fly to Bombay towards the end of July 1967. This was probably the most uncomfortable time of the year in which to experience the monsoon tropical climate. Mrs. Saha's daughter and small son were, like myself, on school vacation, and as their father was busy taking care of a successful restaurant, Joe and I were put in charge of escorting the family to Bombay. Putting aside the medium's warnings, and knowing that I had already taken my precautionary shots, we took off by Kuwait Airways, stopping at Paris, Beirut, Kuwait and Bahrain on our way to India. I was nervous and excited as this was the longest trip I had ever made, and I was not particularly fond of flying, being somewhat prone to panic attacks during take-off and landing. There are times in life when I am sure that ignorance is bliss, and had I known what was in store I might not have had the courage to go.

We landed in Bombay early on a Monday morning after passing through thick blankets of monsoon cloud. As I left the aircraft and descended a flight of metallic steps on to the tarmac, my nostrils were assailed by the humid and peculiar smells of earth, sweat, dung and heated mustard oil. A run-down bus took us to the crowded terminal where every suitcase was opened and eagerly searched by a suspicious customs officer who questioned me about my cine camera and everything else I was carrying. Mrs. Saha and her children were to catch another plane to Calcutta, and so Joe and I left them at the airport. A very sweet Indian couple named Hari and Sangita Ghosh met us. They were Joe's friends and had agreed to accommodate us for several nights in their small garage apartment at Goregaon in North Bombay.

Squeezing our baggage into a taxi we were rushed at breakneck speed through the most crowded streets I had ever seen. The driver constantly changed lanes without signalling, braked abruptly, missed cyclists by inches and truly terrified me! Finally we reached the modest garage home of Hari and Sangita, being immediately introduced to their kind landlord Mr. Sheth, who had a diamond-polishing business which was managed by his young son, Pradip. Mr. Sheth allowed Hari and Sangita to sleep in his spare sitting room, while Joe and I occupied the garage. We were given two wooden-framed string beds with thin mattresses. I had been shown how to tie the mosquito nets to small hooks on the wall and tuck in the nets after climbing inside. I slept bare-chested because of the heat and humidity. During the night, however, one of the strings broke and a portion of the net fell upon my naked body. I slept, deeply, unaware of anything until the following morning, when I discovered to my horror that I had been bitten on every exposed area of flesh by the humming mosquitoes. The property was surrounded by marshland and the heavy rains of the monsoon had left large pools of stagnant water, ideal breeding grounds for the insects. Hundreds of itchy bumps appeared and I was taken to a local doctor for soothing cream and a supply of malaria pills. So much for my first night in Bombay!

Later that week, Joe and I took the air-conditioned train to New Delhi where we were due to meet Joe's mother, Mrs. Labanya Bhowmik and his younger brother Bishnu, who had both travelled from Calcutta to join us. It was an emotional reunion on Delhi station. Mrs. Bhowmik was taller than both her sons, and wore a blue and white sari. Bishnu was a short man, dressed European style in a thin cotton shirt and pants, and was several shades darker in complexion than his brother. Although neither Bishnu nor Mrs. Bhowmik spoke much English, she managed to welcome me as her other son. She too was a schoolteacher by profession and she had booked a room for us all at the Bengali Institute in New Delhi. From there we were to spend a few days seeing the local tourist spots before catching another air-conditioned express all the way east to Calcutta.

New Delhi is a beautiful city of spacious brick-red government buildings, largely designed and built during the period of the 'British Raj'. On a tour of the city, our driver, a turbaned Sikh, pointed out the different landmarks in surprisingly good English. We saw among other things the Red Fort, the Birla Temple, the Secretariat and Parliament House. Everything looked pink. Even the soil surrounding the buildings had a peculiar almost Martian look. The tropical trees and flowers fascinated me. It was all so different from England, and it was incredibly hot!

On August 1st, we caught the 7.25 a.m. Taj Express to the city of Agra, famous for the beautiful marble tomb built by the Mughal Emperor Shah Jahan in memory of his beloved queen Mumtaz. While walking through the gardens of this truly heavenly place I began to feel the beginnings of a headache and a premonition that all was not well. I had covered my head with a small cap, so I doubted that I was developing sunstroke. Saying nothing of my feelings, I joined the others in a taxi ride to the mysterious and deserted city of Fatehpur Sikri, where a tall thin Indian acted as our guide around the ancient ruins. The architecture was stunning and quite different from that of Europe, but an increasing feeling of physical weakness marred my enjoyment.

That night we took another train to the city of Jaipur, travelling by first class sleeping berth. We were literally caught in our pyjamas when the train unexpectedly pulled in at Jaipur station at 4 a.m. Grabbing our suitcases we scrambled quickly on to the platform and managed to find some couches and easy chairs in the special Retiring Rooms made available for travellers. There we were able to sleep until daybreak.

It is a strange feeling being stared at because you are white and in the minority. There is this fascination that Indians have for the European traveller. They will ask you directly about your family, your profession, your earnings and your education. One learns to politely side step the more personal issues. In the market place small children tugged at my clothes, begging for rupees.

While exploring a side street in Jaipur we suddenly came upon a group of ladies clad in the sombre costumes of the Muslim religion. They were chattering quite animatedly, but upon seeing three men they made nervous little squeals and quickly veiled themselves. Through the dark netting that covered their faces I felt myself being scrutinised. I immediately apologised for causing them alarm and was surprised when one of them said in perfect English "We forgive you." Some of the other ladies giggled behind their veils.

Jaipur, the city of pink palaces, is a monument to the imagination of artist and architect. The colours and designs are wonderful to behold. It is a true eastern city and one almost expects to see a wizard taking off on a magic carpet and a turbaned genie arising from one of the giant brass pots on display.

But I was in serious trouble. I had the beginning of 'Delhi belly' and only just reached a somewhat public latrine in time to squat on two small platforms over a dark and smelly hole in the ground.

On the night train back to Delhi, I spent most of my time in the stainless steel bathroom, either throwing up or voiding my bowels, and with each trip down the corridor feeling weaker and weaker. The Bhowmik family was very concerned and we obtained medication at a dispensary in New Delhi.

At 5.30 p.m. on 4th August we caught the air-conditioned train to Calcutta. The carriage was so highly refrigerated that in addition to my bout of dysentery I arrived at Howrah Station, Calcutta, the following evening with a bad cold! The train was four hours late because of people sitting on the track demonstrating against the food crisis. I learned that the Bengalis are very political people. Many are highly educated and speak excellent English, albeit with a strong accent. Some of the younger men spoke with such rapid machine-gun delivery that I had to pay close attention at all times. The Bengali ladies were very sweet and quite emotional.

Mrs. Bhowmik made me welcome in her small flat-roofed home. Joe and I slept in a bedroom that had been added to the roof area. People in Calcutta build their houses gradually according to their financial status. Looking down from the rooftop I could see a small marshy area around which grew banana trees and coconut palms. The place was infested with mosquitoes. All the drains were open and ran alongside the narrow streets.

I was taken to see a rather morose little Bengali doctor who commented that I was visiting India at the wrong time of year. He prescribed medication, and although I was drinking only boiled water, and eating carefully prepared food, I continued to have the runs. It was an effort to drag one foot in front of the other. I lost a lot of weight. Yet I still managed to visit a number of tourist spots like the Victoria Memorial and the Calcutta Botanical Gardens, where I was able to see the largest Banyan tree in Asia. I remember also touching the leaves of small Mimosa plants and watching them suddenly fold up. The exotic perfumes from the flowering trees also captivated me. I saw around me great beauty and great ugliness. Calcutta is truly a city of contrasts.

One day a snake charmer visited the street and all the neighbourhood children gathered to watch him open up some baskets to allow large cobras to emerge and sway rhythmically as he played his mysterious pipes. The snakes glided out from the baskets in a pattern, like spokes from a wheel, and when the charmer tapped his foot they changed direction obediently. The entertainment lasted about fifteen minutes and a small ragged boy went around collecting donations from the crowd.

The people were kind and friendly and eager to escort us wherever we wished to go. I was impressed by their willingness to invite a white man into their homes and to offer sweets and hot tea. I felt much love and acceptance from these people who were all too familiar with food rationing and the need for careful budgeting. Indians are, through necessity,

175

very money-minded and seem to be possessed of a natural wisdom and a philosophical approach to everything. Of course there is bribery and corruption in high places, but the ordinary people of Calcutta had a most loveable quality and were extremely warm and hospitable. The constant beggars tugging at my sleeve initially irritated me, but my innate sense of compassion triumphed, and I soon learned to carry a pocketful of small change in order to satisfy them. Many tiny children get sent out on to the streets as professional beggars by their parents, and it becomes difficult for Europeans to ignore the upturned pleading faces of these desperate souls. It was easy to understand how Communism gained a stronghold in West Bengal. Many of the people were so utterly poor that they were prepared to embrace anything that promised them a fair share of the existing wealth. Never did such a city cry out with such agony for charitable actions. Fortunately, Mother Theresa responded and so did many others from the Hindu community who worked tirelessly behind the scenes to alleviate distress without achieving fame. One day, I am sure their service to their less privileged brethren will be richly rewarded in the world to come.

During my stay in Calcutta my unpredictable health somehow accentuated my psychic ability, and we actually had a séance at Mrs. Bhowmik's home, being visited by an Anglo-Indian family who had relatives in Australia. They were seeking permission to emigrate and sought information about when this would occur. I gave them a date and various names of relatives who had passed over, and it was about a year later that I heard from them in Australia. My prediction had been absolutely correct and they were now happily settled with their relatives down under.

While visiting his family, Joe decided to go ahead with a petition to bring another small brother Nilambu to England, so that the family could be somewhat relieved financially. This was a major decision, but the Bhowmik family was wholeheartedly in agreement with it. Nilambu was a quiet, very thin little boy of eight who obviously liked us and seemed pleased that his older brother wanted to take responsibility for him.

A year later we were to meet this tiny child at Heathrow airport for the beginning of his new life in London. I was to teach him English and prepare him for school. Mrs. Bhowmik was delighted that Nilambu had this golden opportunity to escape from the poverty of Calcutta. It was to be quite a challenge taking on some of the responsibility of a small child, but I was about to enter teachers' training college and Nilambu was to be my first case study. Later, I wrote a paper on the teaching of English to immigrant children in the London Borough of Waltham Forest. Thanks to Nilambu I was getting first-hand experience at doing this. Quite soon Nilambu had his name Anglicised to the more easily recognised one of 'Neil.' I grew to love this small boy with dark brown eyes and his quiet, shy personality. I think he came to regard me as a surrogate parent and for many years we had an extremely good relationship. Neil is now happily settled in Australia with his attractive wife Susan and they have two beautiful daughters.

Above: One of the many Indian temples I visited. Each one had its own unique style of elaborate carvings and statues.

Below: With the Mukherjee family on the beach at Somnath.

22.

I could write a complete book about my experiences in North London as a schoolteacher, but that is not the focus of this autobiography. However, while teaching I was often able to surprise some of the children by my knowledge of events around them, simply by holding one of their pens or books. On one occasion I told a child that I thought her mother's friend had won some money at Bingo. She absolutely denied this, but on returning to school the next day she informed me with utter amazement that what I had predicted had occurred that very evening. Several children in the class said that I must be a kind of wizard, and I was known by some of the more intelligent children as 'the telepathic teacher.' One tall, troubled boy of fifteen said I gave him the creeps when I mentioned that he had just had a new red lampshade put in his bedroom.

These classroom games would take place at the end of a lesson if we had a few moments to spare. I would usually say to the children that we all needed to watch our thinking because bad thoughts could lead to bad actions. I demonstrated that sometimes people's thoughts could be read, and I admit to sometimes using my 'powers' in order to keep better control in my classroom. Adolescents can be notoriously difficult to teach, and it seems that a certain amount of entertainment must also accompany their learning process. There is no doubt that a teacher with personality and a good sense of humour is often going to have better success than one who is dry and lifeless.

Tuesday November 28th, 1972 is a date I will never forget. Some really extraordinary things happened. One event was very shocking, the other event most inspiring. If it could be called a meaningful day, that would still be an understatement. I had arranged to take the afternoon off school as I had booked my first sitting with the famous London independent voice medium, Mr. Leslie Flint. I had heard so much about Leslie from other people that I had finally decided to experience one of his séances for myself. However, I had to get through a morning of teaching at the Walthamstow school where I was employed.

I was enjoying my cup of tea during the morning break period, when I was approached by two of the young prefects who were complaining that a thirteen-year-old girl had refused to go outside on to the playground in spite of repeated requests. I approached the girl who was skulking around in the front lobby and told her that she must follow the rules and go outside. Although it was a pleasant day the girl was determined not to leave the lobby. When another teacher also told her to go outside she began swearing at us. I took her gently but firmly by both arms and escorted her through the double swing doors into the quadrangle, while she squealed loudly that I should take my 'bleeding hands' off her. After kicking the door and making a great commotion, she then began crossing the quadrangle to another set of entrance doors by a cloakroom. She was about to re-enter the school when the other teacher and I again intercepted her. This time she was in tears and appeared to be almost hysterical. Before we could question her about why she was so reluctant to be in the playground, she grabbed her coat from the cloakroom, used more foul language and ran out of another door. She had obviously gone home. She was not popular with the other children, but she was as strong as an ox and would have been a formidable opponent in a fight.

After break, I was teaching a very pleasant first year class in my upstairs room. The children were doing their written work and all was quiet and peaceful. Suddenly my classroom door burst open and a woman with a loud, raucous voice demanded to know whether I was "Mr. Urst." When I acknowledged this fact she then demanded that I step out on to the landing. I noticed that a younger woman, who had a large German shepherd dog on a chain, accompanied her. "Come out 'ere!" the raucous woman screamed. Sensing big trouble I quickly unlocked another door at the rear of my classroom. This door led into the geography room where my friend Harry was teaching a class. I requested that Harry come quickly into my room as a witness. When the angry woman saw this, she strode down the aisle and grabbed hold of me, her sharp fingernails flashing in front of my face. She was about to claw me viciously when her upraised hand was grabbed quickly by the headmaster who had suddenly entered the room. I was so shocked by the incident that I was physically trembling. The children in my class looked petrified. The woman was escorted away and luckily the bell soon rang for the end of the lesson.

Subsequently, with legal aid from the National Union of Teachers, I took the mother to Court, where looking quite sheepish she made an apology through her solicitor. The case had a small write-up in the Stratford Express newspaper and the girl was placed in an alternative school. When it was first announced that the girl was being transferred, I was cheered loudly in the staff room by many of the teachers who had experienced trouble from her. But I jump ahead of my story.

That afternoon, still feeling a little shaken from my encounter with the angry mother and the German shepherd, I met Joe, and together we proceeded to the address of Leslie Flint in Westbourne Terrace, and rang the bell by the side of the heavy, antique front door.

After a few moments, a younger round-faced man with glasses, who seemed to have a permanent smirk, answered the door. This was Bram Rogers, who was Leslie's close friend and assistant. In a somewhat theatrical voice he announced that we should follow him downstairs where the sitting would be held. While standing in the basement passageway we saw a fairly short, portly gentleman with a shock of thick, silvery hair emerge from a bedroom. He introduced himself in a deep and resonant voice as Leslie Flint. A number of other people were also waiting to join the sitting, and Leslie escorted us all into a medium-sized room that contained a couple of large sofas and several armchairs. I noticed a microphone on a tall stand in front of one armchair and a large reel-to-reel tape recorder nearby. I saw Joe glancing cautiously around the room looking for evidence of paraphernalia that might have been used to create mysterious voices. He was not yet convinced that all this was above board, but as this was his first encounter with physical mediumship he was naturally guarded and suspicious.

Around the walls of the beautifully decorated room were numerous signed photographs of movie and theatrical celebrities. I noticed among others, pictures of the Welsh actor and composer Ivor Novello and the American screen-goddess, Mae West. Later, I learned that Leslie had given sittings to both of them as well as to many other celebrities.

After Joe and I were seated on a large sofa opposite the medium and the other sitters had taken their places, Joe pulled out a large Kodak envelope containing a blank photographic plate that a friend had given him to be placed on the séance room floor. Leslie readily agreed to this spur-of-the-moment experiment which was to test the ability of the spirits to create 'psychic images' on the photographic plate. The lights were extinguished and Leslie asked us to remove the plate from the dark envelope and to put it on the floor at our feet. After Joe had done this, Leslie began chatting generally to the group about his gift and how sometimes it worked and sometimes it didn't.

Ten minutes passed and eventually some whispering was heard in the air just above Leslie's head. The medium commented that it did not sound like his Cockney boy guide, Mickey. He wondered whether it was a spirit trying to speak "in Hindustani" to Joe. He asked Joe to speak in his own language (Bengali) and Joe immediately obliged. The whispered response could not be understood and Joe stated that the language was unknown to him.

Almost immediately the prepubescent voice of Mickey spoke and addressed one of the ladies with whom he seemed to be familiar. Mickey was in a joking mood and commented that she'd brought her "old man" with her. The lady confirmed this and then Mickey asked her about the hotel that she owned. In the ensuing conversation it became obvious that she was hoping Mickey could help her buy another hotel in Spain. Mickey wisely said "You'll have to give me time to think about that one…I don't want to rush you into something like that, mate!"

Soon a man's voice could be heard calling out "Lily…I want to speak to Lily." A lady with a north-country accent responded that she was Lily. The voice claimed to be that of her father. After a few moments of general conversation that was not very evidential, Lily's father commented that he had his wife there also waiting to speak. Then the spirit gave several names and these were immediately recognised by Lily. She explained to her deaf husband, who was sitting beside her that both his parents were also there trying to speak. Mickey clinched the identity by saying "There's someone here called John Jones and he's here with Annie Jones...and they both send their love and blessings to you, your mum and dad." The deaf man was obviously pleased that his dead parents' names had been mentioned. Mickey's voice became loud and somewhat shrill when he spoke directly to the deaf husband. Mickey told him about a dead son who had died in an accident many years previously. This was correct.

"Your boy tells me that in your pocket you've got some photographs," Mickey said.

The deaf husband seemed a little vague and Lily had to confirm this by saying, "You've got several in your wallet, haven't you?"

Finally the husband admitted "Oh yes, I think I have."

Mickey immediately snapped: "What do you mean 'you think'? Don't you damn well know what you've got in your pocket?"

The husband tried to defend his vagueness by saying that he had not put the photographs in his pocket that day, but had only carried them with him. Mickey commented "You've changed your coat and you put them in your pocket."

Finally the deaf man admitted that this was true. Mickey continued by telling the man that his dead son was saying that "some buttons had to be done...and there was something that had to be altered, to do with a suit."

Lily immediately confirmed this information and then Mickey told her that her birthday was just after Christmas. She replied that it was on January 3rd.

Soon their dead son Teddy was speaking in the room. I give a transcript of their amazing conversation for the benefit of other parents who may have lost children.

Male Voice (from the air): Hello, Mum.

Lily: Hello! Is that Teddy?

Teddy: Yes, Teddy speaking. Hello, Dad.

Deaf husband: Hello Ted! It's amazing!

Teddy: I'm so glad that you've come to speak to me. I was telling the little boy about the suit that was altered.

Lily: Yes.

Teddy: Mum, how are you?

Lily: I'm very well.

Teddy: You know I'm well and happy. You know I come and see you practically every day.

Lily: Yes. You've grown up, haven't you Teddy?

Teddy: Well, I'm not a little boy anymore, and if you could see me you'd be surprised. I look about twenty-one or twenty-two now, I suppose. I'm not a child you know.

Lily: No, well I didn't think you would be.

Teddy: Don't think of me as miles away. I'm near you. Every day I come and see you and Dad. Can you hear me?

Lily: Yes, very well.

Teddy: Oh dear! I can't think what to say. I'm so excited. Oh, Mum, I'm so happy. Don't worry about any of us. Gran spoke to you, and Granddad. I know I could do this better, but I'm doing my best.

Lily: Oh, you're very clear.

Teddy then made some reference to a bike, but his mother did not understand. Mickey intervened and explained that Teddy had had no time to enjoy the tricycle that had been given to him as a small child.

Lily: Well that could very well be. He was seven, Mickey, and he died like you did.

Teddy: Mum, you remember that bike?

Lily: Yes, you had a tricycle.

Teddy: I didn't have much chance to get a ride on it.

Lily: No, you didn't.

Teddy: I have no regrets now…It all happened so suddenly. Mum, what have you done with the lock of hair?

Lily: Oh, I've still got…

Teddy: In the envelope.

Lily: I've still got it.

Teddy: You've got it still in that box?

Lily: Yes, yes.

Teddy: With those other bits and pieces.

Lily: Oh, yes.

Teddy: And mum, you know I was promised a watch.

Lily: Yes, you may have been, Teddy. It's a long time ago.

Teddy: Mum, I was with you the other day when you went down to that place in the country.

Lily: Oh, yes?

Teddy: You know the place I mean?

Lily (Being cautious): No, I can't just think of it.

Teddy: Dad was with you.

Lily: Well, we've been to many places and you could be with us.

Mickey (Suddenly interrupting): But lady, have you fairly recently been down into the country to Sussex?

Lily: Yes, we're going to Sussex after this…

Mickey: Yes, because he keeps talking about going to Sussex, you see.

Lily: Yes, that's very good because…

Mickey: And you're going there today are you?

Lily: His sister lives in Sussex.

After further conversation about the relatives in Sussex, Mickey told the deaf husband that he had been treated at the hospital during the last year for haemorrhoids. Lily confirmed this. Mickey then described the presence of a spirit man who had once lived in a Milton Road. The deaf husband remembered that one of his uncles had lived at such an address many years previously. Mickey also mentioned a Florence Webb who had once been the man's neighbour, but he was unable to remember her.

At that point the tape ran out in my portable recorder, and I quickly opened the flap in the dark to change over the tape. As I did this, Mickey was on to it immediately:

Mickey: What are you doing with that thing, fidget-assing about?

Brian Hurst: Oh sorry! It's the cassette. I beg your pardon.

Mickey: All right, carry on cock!

Brian Hurst: I'm taking a recording of your voice.

Mickey: Oh blimey!

Brian Hurst: I can hear every word. It's marvellous!

Mickey: Oh, well there's no point in bloody well coming if you can't hear nothing!

(General laughter)

Leslie Flint: Mickey, you're shocking!

Another lady: Mickey, you're funny!

Mickey: Well, you know. I suppose some people expect me to be all holy, but I ain't. I'm me self! I don't pretend to be spiritual, not in the sense that some people think. I mean, I'm not a bad person, but I ain't high-falutin' like some of 'em. Some of 'em give you the pip!"

Mickey then made mention of someone who had known me when I was connected with a shop. The person was not named but I was given the message that I would be helped when I started up something on my own, later in life. Mickey then went on to speak to another woman named Betty who also wanted to go and live in Spain. In a joking manner he told her that she would need quite a bit of money to live abroad. Apart from light-hearted banter, no evidential facts were given to Betty or her husband that accompanied her.

Mickey then became aware of the spirit of a young man who had committed suicide. The young man told Mickey that he had met me once when I had been to a party in London. He said his name was Peter and that he had killed himself because of an unhappy love affair. He said that he had come from Epsom in Surrey and used to frequent a pub called 'The Cricketers.' Later he moved to London, where he apparently killed himself. I could not place this man at all.

There was a long silence and then a deep male voice began speaking to me with a distinct French accent. He gave the name of Andre and said that he had been in the spirit world a very long time. He continued: "I have great hope that I may be of some help and service to you. You have much power, of which you know nothing. This can be developed and used, and at a later date when it is possible, I and other souls here will manifest and use you, but at the moment it is not possible, for you are very unsettled, but this will not last. Soon there will be change for you, which will benefit you materially and you will have more opportunity to consider these things."

I thought about the way in which I had been attacked in my classroom that morning and I had already considered the possibility of leaving London with its rowdy adolescents and taking a teaching job out in India. I mentioned my desire to go abroad and was told that this was not immediately possible.

"Try to be patient," Andre said, "But by the coming year, you will see the beginning of the plan."

I asked Andre when he had first known me. He said it was when I was a little boy. Then he continued with some strange information: "I want you to know that we have known each other in a previous incarnation...I have impressed you, and I will impress other people who do not know anything about you. Miles away from this house I will come to you in a strange way, so it will seem. I will impress certain people to talk to you about me. This I promise."

I thanked him. He continued:

"You will have confirmation of these things. You have been chosen by this world of spirit to do certain work in your world. At the moment it is not possible, the way has yet to be straight for you, but it will be done. Leave it to the power of the spirit, which is all around and about you. I and other souls here will manifest, and in due course and time you will see how clear the path is."

Andre's voice faded away and I found myself quite overwhelmed by this strange message and his promise of coming to me in a faraway place. Immediately I thought of the French spirit guide I had seen in the movie many years previously, the man who had taken the pilot up the stairway to heaven while his brain was receiving surgery on earth. Now I also had a French guide who had promised to help me. Although I had not received any evidential message from a close family member, I was totally blown away by what had come through. Afterwards I wondered why there had been no reference to the shocking event of that morning, but upon analysis it seemed possible that no spirit person had been with me at the time, and therefore the communicators probably had no knowledge of the event. To those mediums who say, "Your loved ones are with you all the time" I find myself replying "Baloney!" It is of course possible that the confrontation was known about but not mentioned for fear of spoiling the harmony within the séance room.

The incredible voice séance continued for another three quarters of an hour, but I was not addressed by any other entity.

When the meeting finally closed, Joe was reminded to return the photographic plate to its dark envelope. Upon subsequent examination by a photographer friend, no image was found upon the plate. I realise now that special teams of spirits are necessary for the production of any such images, and psychic photography was definitely not the focus of Leslie's mediumship. Later in my life I was to meet mediums who did have the extraordinary ability to be the catalysts for most incredible photographic phenomena. I will discuss these gifted people in a later chapter.

23

My daily life as a schoolteacher in Walthamstow left me with little energy to pursue the further development of my mediumship. I had helped Neil to acquire a greater understanding of the English language and I also did some private tuitions. Teaching these children stimulated my interest in phonic methods and helped me appreciate the difficulties that many children experience in mastering the language. However, I still toyed with the idea of teaching abroad.

Meanwhile Neil's brother Joe had been successful as a textile designer and his beautiful motif "Pageant" had been voted the top-selling design at Heal's Fabrics in Tottenham Court Road. Joe worked on a sloping desk that I had built for him in a small upstairs bedroom of his house and produced a number of highly colourful and very exotic designs which, in my opinion, could easily compete with those of Victorian artist William Morris.

One day Joe asked whether I would assist him in setting up an exhibition of Indian Art at the Camden Arts Centre in North London. Hallam Tennyson, a broadcaster and great grandson of the famous poet Alfred Lord Tennyson, was also involved in the exhibition. As it was a weekend, Neil accompanied us, and Hallam's father, Sir Charles Tennyson, offered to take the boy to a cartoon theatre while we adults worked on the setting up of the display. Later, at the Tennyson home in Highgate, Sir Charles, an elderly gentleman of medium height, wearing small round spectacles, was kind enough to take me into his room and show me autographed copies of poems by his famous grandfather. It was a memorable visit to the home of a celebrated family. Hallam Tennyson had spent some time in Calcutta and was consequently most familiar with the culture of West Bengal. He had taken a liking to Joe's work and wanted to include some of it in the showcases.

Dame Sybil Thorndike, the wonderful actress for whom George Bernard Shaw had written his play *St. Joan*, opened the exhibition. She stood before us with commanding presence and proceeded to joke about her husband's interest in automobiles! She was married to the well-known actor Sir Lewis Casson. With dramatic delivery and beautiful diction she described how they had sometimes "fought like two tigers on the banks of the Ganges" (Both were Scorpio), and how he would "jump right down my throat if I dared to suggest what might be wrong with a spluttering engine." Her broad, aquiline features surveyed the audience with warmth, and her anecdotes often directed against herself, endeared her to the enthralled crowd. It was the second time I had met her.

During my Guildhall days I had worked at the Globe Theatre in Shaftesbury Avenue where both Dame Sybil and Sir Lewis were appearing in '*Eighty in the Shade*' by Clemence Dane. I had gone backstage and introduced myself, presenting her with a bouquet of flowers. She had been charming and gracious and they had both autographed my programme. She later wrote me a little 'thank you' note, which I still possess. At the Camden Arts Centre she had lost none of her charisma and the Exhibition was a great success.

Early in 1973 another Bengali designer came to the front door of our small terraced house in Forest Gate. He had been sent by the Calico Mills in Ahmedabad to scout for talent overseas. The Sarabhai family then owned the textile mills and they needed someone to be in charge of a new design studio. They had heard about Joe's beautiful designs and were desirous of employing him. The talent scout told Joe that Calico Mills would be happy to provide all of us with accommodation for a few days if we wished to visit Ahmedabad to meet the design team. Suhrid Sarabhai happened to be at college in Cambridge and we finalised arrangements through him to again visit India that summer. I was determined that this time I would take every precaution to avoid sickness. I had my shots and a good supply of malaria pills and medicine for diarrhoea. I vowed that no unboiled water would touch my lips. This time, fourteen-year-old Neil was to accompany the two of us on our return to India, so that he could once again see his family after our business part of the trip was ended.

Ahmedabad is a desert city about three hundred miles north of Bombay. It lies close to the tropic of Cancer and is dissected by the enormous River Sabarmati. The local language is Gujarati but most educated people can speak English. The local Hindu

195

population was mostly vegetarian and on the outskirts of the ancient city were a number of housing societies in which members of the various branches of Hinduism (and Christianity) tended to live. The inner city had many ancient buildings with beautiful carved wooden decorations and mazes of tiny streets known as 'poles'. The inner city was also quite dirty, crowded and smelly from camel, donkey and goat urine being heated by the tropical sun. There was the constant noisy honking of taxis and auto rickshaws, and the danger of tripping on broken flagstones in neglected footpaths damaged by the roots of Banyan trees.

Indians appear to have rather mixed attitudes towards the British. Several older men confronted me with the fact that the British Raj had done some rather terrible things in its time. I immediately agreed with them and added "Yes, I'm very sorry about that, but none of *my* family was involved in the suppression of freedom in India." After those initial remarks, the older men showed greater friendliness and respect for me and I had no further trouble in these political discussions.

Joe, Neil and I stayed for several days at the Calico Mill Guesthouse where we were treated most hospitably. We met various members of the millionaire Sarabhai family: Gautram, Gira, his energetic sister, and the charming Suhrid, who had been studying in Cambridge University. I expressed my interest in teaching overseas, and it was quickly suggested that I might be able to assist another relative who ran a private English-medium school named Shreyas. Her name was Lena Mangaldas and she was planning to have a Shakespeare festival the following year at her beautiful school which was situated on a tree-covered hill to the north of the city of Ahmedabad.

I met Lenaben[3] (as she was known) a number of times and discussed how the festival might be organised. Lenaben was a rather regal, round-faced lady, beautifully dressed in the Indian style and obviously used to an authoritative role in most affairs. When I knew that she was a Leo, it helped me to understand her. She seemed to find me acceptable and it was arranged for me to return to India the following January and to be employed as a teacher at the school.

Meanwhile Joe had agreed to accept the position as Head of the new design studio at Calico Mills. We were introduced to Mr. Bijoy Mohanty, a round-faced man from the State of Orissa, who was cataloguing the contents of the Calico Museum of Textiles. He was most friendly and told us that his Irish wife and young daughter, who had suffered from polio, were obliged to stay back in Orissa to take care of the family home while he was on this assignment. He was temporarily sharing a large box-like house with another employee of the Museum. The two-storey flat roofed residence was situated in the Shardar Nagar Building Society on the north side of the Sabarmati River. It was agreed that we would also move into this ample accommodation upon our return to India the following January.

197

Feeling confident that we both had jobs and a place to live upon our return, we left Ahmedabad and travelled by train to Patna in Central India where we were again to meet Mrs. Bhowmik and her son Bishnu for further sight-seeing. Mrs. Bhowmik had not seen her young son Neil for almost five years. He was growing into a tall, slender teenage boy with thick curly black hair. He was quiet, well-behaved and never any problem, fitting in with the arrangements to return to India without any apparent regret.

To my relief I remained in good health throughout our travels to monsoon-flooded Patna, on the banks of the raging Ganges. The hotel was rather primitive, with plumbing that left much to be desired. The streets were knee-deep in water. We stayed only one night, then left for a nearby hill station of Rajgir. There I had a terrifying ride in a single chair lift to the top of a mountain. The ground literally dropped away and I found myself suspended in space over a gaping chasm while the wind gently swayed the ascending chair. I have never liked heights and I was petrified by this experience. The beautiful temple on the mountain top was well worth the visit but on the descent, I was quite terrified of again swinging in space suspended over the deep chasm below.

We also visited Nalanda and Bhagalpur where the brother of one of our friends from London resided. Bonku Sinha was happy to see us. He lived with his attractive young wife and elderly mother in a modest house on the outskirts of town. Meeting us at the station he took us by rickshaw to the family home.

After a tasty Indian meal we talked into the small hours. Later, the mosquito nets were erected around the beds and I settled in to a good night's rest.

Early the next morning, shouts and screams from outside awaked me. Looking through the iron bars at the window I was greeted by a shocking scene. The large gateway of the opposite house was wide open, and there was a small crowd of people moving about excitedly, while a couple of policemen in shorts carrying bamboo canes tried to keep order. The inner door of the house was also open and I could clearly see the lifeless body of a young woman swinging from a ceiling fan. She had apparently taken her own life the previous night. Bonku was concerned that I stay out of sight. He didn't want the superstitious people to associate my visit to the village with bad luck. Later that day I did take a walk down to the Ganges, where to my utter astonishment, I ran straight into the father of the deceased girl. He had erected a small altar by the river and he was praying and chanting and crying bitterly. He looked up at me and said in perfect English "Everyone is blaming me. I am a very unhappy man. I tried to get my daughter married to a good boy. She opposed my wishes and now this terrible thing has happened. What can I do? Everyone hates me!"

I tried to speak comforting words to the distressed man. I put my arm around him and he continued crying on my shoulder. I remember saying that there was definitely life after death, and that his unhappy daughter had moved on to the next level where she would get help and counselling. He was full of remorse for his stubborn refusal to accept her rejection of the arranged marriage. I felt deeply sorry for him and also for the young Indian girl who had been driven to such a drastic course of action. I had heard dramatic stories of Indian women taking their own lives, but never thought that I would actually witness such an event at close quarters. I said some prayers in English for the distraught family and sadly continued my walk by the sacred river. The grieving father seemed oddly touched by my concern and stared after me like I was a visitor from another planet.

During this dramatic trip we also visited Bodha Gaya where history relates that Buddha received his enlightenment while meditating under the Bodhi tree. There was a beauty and serenity about the whole place that was not even disturbed by the vendors and people with cooking pots boiling masala-laced tea and calling "char" in their monotonous voices to the passing tourists. I found myself absorbing the unique atmosphere of this holy place. Then, accompanied by Bonku, we returned to Calcutta by train for a few days.

Joe had apparently decided that Neil should remain in India until our return the following January. I was not at all happy with that idea as I could see the pained expression on the boy's face. He felt like he was being abandoned. Bonku and his wife (both good people) had agreed to lodge Neil at their home in Bihar, so that he could attend school there and begin to learn Hindi. I seriously questioned the wisdom of that scheme, as I knew that it would be quite a traumatic change. Neil hardly knew the young Indian couple, and when Bonku and Neil left Calcutta by train, Neil was weeping uncontrollably as he said goodbye to me. He only wanted to return to England with me, but I was powerless to do anything, as I was not his legal guardian. It was a painful and difficult situation and Joe succeeded in alienating a number of people by his decision at that time. Shortly after we had returned to England, Neil's mother visited Bihar and took her son back to Calcutta. He remained there until our return to India the following January.

Above: Bonku's elderly mother and wife preparing food for
us. The conditions appear primitive but the vegetarian meal
was excellent. We were made most welcome.

24.

In December 1973 I quit my teaching job in London and was all set to leave for India. I began collecting Shakespearean material and recordings of Elizabethan music ready for the Festival that Lenaben planned to organise at Shreyas School. Reluctantly, Joe sold the house in Forest Gate and began crating up many of his household possessions for shipment to Bombay. I also sent packages of books for my future use as a teacher. After again visiting Calcutta and bringing Neil back we settled with the help of Calico Mills into the large box-like concrete residence in Shardar Nagar Society. Smiling Mr. Mohanty greeted us, glad of company, as the other Calico employee had moved out a short time earlier.

We were soon introduced to our pleasant neighbours, Mr. & Mrs. Trivedi and their four young sons. All of them spoke some English and made me feel most welcome. Gaurang, the middle son, took me to buy a bicycle, as I needed transportation to the nearby Shreyas School. We also required a ration card to make us eligible for milk delivery and we had to sign an Agreement with the housing society that we would not eat meat while residing there as all people in that society were vegetarians. I had no problem with this as I had been a vegetarian for some years, but Joe and Neil had been used to eating mutton and fish, so it was probably quite a sacrifice for them.

Neither of us was aware of the dangerous situation that was to arise upon reaching Ahmedabad. Civil strife had broken out. The left-wing students were revolting against the central government and its presumed corruption. Riots were taking place in the streets and all the schools were suddenly closed. There was a situation of grave emergency. Some dissenters had been shot and I was later to see a number of dead bodies lying by the railroad.

Lenaben, the Principal of Shreyas School apologetically explained that the Shakespeare Festival could not take place. As she had some residential students from Africa (Indian children from wealthy families) she had to devise some activities for them which would not appear to be infringing the student rule that no schools were to be open. She was in a very difficult position. News leaked out that Lenaben had a foreign teacher (myself) and that some educational activities were being conducted against the orders of the student body.

One day I was being shown around the beautiful campus, which was situated on top of a hill, when news reached us that the students were marching towards the school and were intent upon making mischief. We also heard that armed police were watching the school from another part of the compound. It looked like a very tense situation.

Lenaben ordered that the Library building be closed securely and the barred windows be shuttered. Some frightened teachers took shelter inside the upstairs library, while others removed items from the downstairs office. I decided to remain at some distance and observe events from under the shade of some trees. I was however soon spotted and the students moved in my direction.

Approaching one of the leaders, I was psychically impressed to put my arm around him and confidentially whisper into his ear that the school really was closed and I was merely there on a visit. To my relief, he listened calmly. I urged that there be no violence as armed police were outside the campus and I didn't wish to see anyone shot. The man appeared to understand me and said something in Gujarati to his colleagues. Lenaben then emerged from behind the office and bravely went forward to meet the student leaders, smilingly informing them that they were most welcome to her school. At that moment, agitators in the crowd began picking up stones and throwing them at the school notice boards. A deflected stone narrowly missed Lenaben's face, though nothing was hurled in my direction.

I watched with concern as a number of hotheads ran up the steps to the library and began throwing themselves against the barricaded doors. Fortunately the doors held firm and the students eventually gave up on their efforts. I learned later that they would have destroyed most of the books had they gained admission. They had done a similar thing at another school, such was the level of their rage and frustration.

Lenaben watched helplessly as her beautiful car parked behind the office was systematically vandalised. I realised there was nothing further I could do to help. The students would not physically harm her because she was a woman and most Hindus are taught to respect the female sex. Quietly I slipped away, saddened that my words of peace had been ineffective.

Here, I should explain that in Gujarat the suffix 'ben' is always respectively added to a woman's name, implying that she is a 'sister.' Hence: 'Lenaben.' In a similar way 'bhai' is attached to a man's name implying that he is a 'brother.' I was fascinated by this custom and willingly agreed to be called 'Brianbhai.'

Meanwhile Joe was put in charge of a new design studio at Calico Mill. Neil waited to be enrolled in an English medium school that had a suitable vacancy and Lenaben, realising that she could not employ me at Shreyas, asked whether I would mind acting as personal tutor to her young grandsons Arjun and Abhay Mangaldas who both needed help with their English. While all this was being arranged, Neil and I had some free afternoons, during which we would take a rickshaw and complete a few errands, at the same time seeing something of the ancient city of Ahmedabad. It was on one such afternoon that a very strange thing occurred.

The house in which we lived had a marble staircase that descended into the living room. Mr. Mohanty occupied the upstairs room with its adjoining bathroom and we had use of the complete ground floor. Neil and I had just finished drinking our afternoon tea in the front sitting room and were getting ready to leave the house. Unlike Western-type homes the front door had a long sliding bolt that had to be secured by a padlock upon leaving the house. While we were at home, this padlock and key were always kept on a small round table at the foot of the marble staircase. Neil approached the table and picked up the padlock. To his surprise the small key fell out in two pieces upon the table. Curiously he held the two parts of the key together to find that they had been bent and broken at an angle of ninety degrees. When he showed me this I asked whether he had been messing around with the key and had accidentally broken it. His astonished denial made me realise he was telling the truth. Besides it was a strong metal key and would have been most difficult to break without pliers. We were both extremely puzzled by this strange event. Fortunately we had a spare padlock and used it to secure the house before we went on our errands.

That evening Joe returned from Calico Mill waving the March 6th edition of an American newsmagazine. "I thought you might like to read this," he said, entering the house, "There's an article about Uri Geller bending keys."

We had not had any time to tell Joe about the fate of our own front door key. Astonished by his words, I grabbed the magazine and opened it straight at a picture of Uri Geller holding a bent key. The synchronicity of this event was quite astonishing. Neil then took Joe to the round table and showed him what had happened that very afternoon. Excited and puzzled, we discussed psychic phenomena well into the evening.

However that was not the end of it! The next morning I needed my bicycle to make a short trip. Neil and I stored our cycles in a long closet behind the kitchen for security. I entered the gloomy closet and tried to wheel my bicycle backward into the kitchen. Something was wrong. The machine would not move. Looking down at the pedal I was quite shocked to see that *the main shaft to which the pedal was attached had been bent inwards at an angle of forty-five degrees*, making the bicycle unusable in its present condition. Considerable force must have been used against that strong metal shaft, yet no one had been anywhere near that closet since I had placed my bicycle there the previous day. Utterly amazed, I suddenly remembered the Leslie Flint séance in London where Andre, the Frenchman, had promised that he would come to me in a very strange way thousands of miles from that house. Could this be Andre keeping his promise? If so, it certainly was a very strange way of doing it.

Above: My first Indian home at 78, Sharda Nagar Society, Ahmedabad, where the strange phenomena occurred. I slept on the front upstairs balcony under a mosquito net and could wave to Ramesh's family who lived opposite me and slept on their roof during the very hot season. Some years later the house was demolished and rebuilt as it was rumoured to be haunted. After the many séances we held there I am not surprised.

25.

In order to use the new bicycle I had bought, I first had to straighten the right crankshaft from its extraordinary position where it was touching the chain ring. I had never seen such a thing in my whole life and racked my brains for a possible meaning to this event. Were hostile spirits watching the house and did they disapprove of me as a foreigner? Or was some benevolent soul afraid I might get killed while riding a bicycle on the crowded streets of Ahmedabad?

"Look, you guys!" I muttered to the powers that be, "I need transportation and don't have money to buy a car, even if they would sell me one. I just have to ride this bicycle. Understand?"

Then I lifted the machine and took it to the 'open chock' at the front of the house. I had learned that term from the neighbours who used the word 'chock' for a covered tiled area near the front door that was the equivalent of an open porch.

When I began banging the crankshaft with a hammer, two of the Trivedi boys popped their heads over the adjoining wall and asked what I was doing. I was honest and told them that something very strange had happened to my bicycle. They were over the wall in a flash, looking wide-eyed at the bent crankshaft. Then I told them about the mysterious breaking of the key on the previous afternoon.

Hemang Trivedi said there were rumours that the house was haunted and that was why the family who owned it did not live there. Before Mr. Mohanty had rented it, the place had been empty for some time. The owner, a Mr. Gokli had said that his family preferred to live in Bombay, which seemed a reasonable explanation for him wishing to let the house. As we were discussing these things, the boy from across the road joined us. He was nineteen-year-old Ramesh Jani, and in broken English he said that he believed in the power of the spirits. He said that his mother Jasuben was actually a medium. My ears pricked up. I had come all this way to India to find myself living opposite another medium? Ramesh said that his father had been married twice. The first wife, a very loving woman named Pushpa had given birth to one son, Harshadbhai, and then she had died. Sometime later Ramesh's father had married Jasuben and she had given birth to several more children, including Ramesh. On frequent occasions Jasuben would fall into trances and the spirit of Pushpa would come through and give messages to the family. What an extraordinary thing, I thought. I was interested in questioning Mrs. Jani, but unfortunately she spoke no English and Ramesh had little command of the language at that time. Eventually I did manage to straighten the bicycle crankshaft and that peculiar event was the talk of the neighbourhood for some days.

When it was known that I studied astrology, various young couples began turning up at my front door anxious to have their horoscope charts compared for compatibility in marriage. There was just one case where I told the young girl to keep looking, as the Indian boy from America with the

Green Card was not right for her. She smiled and said, "I told my father that. Now perhaps he will believe me!" Without going into technicalities, certain signs and planets are compatible while others are not. If one partner's Mars opposes the other's Saturn, they will have a tendency to fight! A Moon/Venus conjunction between the two charts will often indicate romance, but of course there are many other aspects to consider. I believe Astrology is an art based upon a science. It is the art of reading the symbols and interpreting them. I fail to see how it can be called a science because of the many variables present and the unpredictability of human nature. How boring if everything was already planned for us in a precise mathematical manner! I am a staunch believer in free will. We are not slaves to the stars!

While Joe was working at the studio and Neil was at school I often had time in the hot April afternoons to read or relax. The house had no air-conditioning, but each room had a fan. One afternoon I had closed the wooden window shutters and I was sitting at the dining room table in a pair of shorts, contemplating writing a letter to my parents in England. Suddenly an unnatural chill seemed to surround me and I visibly shivered. From previous experience in my work as a medium, I recognised this as a signal of the presence of spirit beings. My arms were suddenly covered with gooseflesh and the hairs stood on end. I looked up, curious to see who might be visiting me. As my gaze wandered over to the yellow shuttered windows with their horizontal iron bars I began to see transparent faces floating in the air. To my surprise I thought I recognised the chubby face of the poet, Samuel Taylor Coleridge and the dark curly hair and distinctive nose of Lord Byron. It was so totally unexpected that I remember drawing in breath quite sharply and staring for some moments into the air. The images seemed to melt away as I tried to see them more clearly. I had not read the works of either poet for some time and I had certainly been occupied with thoughts far removed from poetry. Suddenly, I heard a voice in my head say clearly "Get a pencil and paper."

"What do you want of me?" I asked mentally.

"You will take down what we dictate," the voice replied authoritatively.

I felt a sudden surge of enthusiasm, and said, "If you can give me something of interest, I'll be happy to take it down."

The voice then said: "Sit at two o'clock every day and we will come to you for a short time, as we cannot stay in your world for too long. The composition we will give you will be in modified Spenserian stanzas. It will be the story of 'Cinderella' in verse."

I understood that the Spenserian stanza had been invented by the English Poet Edmund Spenser, who had written a long poem entitled 'The Faery Queen' in honour of Queen Elizabeth the First. I took the pencil in my hand and felt a strange tingling in the top of my head. Almost instantly words and phrases began trickling into my mind. It was like a subliminal whisper. I became totally immersed in what I was doing, and completely unaware of my surroundings as I wrote down the words. I don't think I was in a trance but maybe some kind of 'overshadowing' was taking place. My solar plexus area became very sensitive and I was aware of a feeling of exhilaration and excitement. Certainly some kind of telepathic communication of an extraordinary nature was taking place. Occasionally the voice would interrupt my stream of thought with some disapproving remark like "Rub that out. I don't like it!" I would immediately oblige and erase the offending lines. Two or more completely different lines would then be given to me very quickly. At times I was critical of odd words or phrases and my mind would suggest an alternative. The voice would then cut into my thoughts rather sharply, telling me to leave the composition alone. The communicators kept to their word and remained with me for only a brief period each afternoon, and I would be given at the most only five stanzas a day. Upon completion of stanza 66 the voice said, "That is the end of part one. We will give you more later when conditions are suitable. Wait for our direction." They departed as suddenly as they had arrived. I tried on a number of occasions to recapture the psychic feeling and to call the communicators for further stanzas, but it was not until 1981, when I was a student at California State College in San Bernardino, USA, that I began to receive part two of the Cinderella poem that has now been published. It is a remarkably humorous and atmospheric piece that has delighted all friends who have read it.

My reputation as an English teacher and student of the Occult spread rapidly. I was asked to lecture on English writers at the National Institute of Design in Ahmedabad and I made a number of good friends there. After a short term tutoring the Mangaldas children I was offered a teaching job at The Little Flower Primary and High School. It was an English medium school and most of the classes had over 60 children. I worked in classrooms that had no air-conditioning, but only ceiling fans. Most of the children were in their early teens and were quite delightful: bright, motivated and basically kind. One boy decided he would say rude words in Gujarati, knowing that I did not understand the language. His classmates soon gave him away and he shamefacedly responded to a ticking off. At least the children didn't throw furniture at me. During a teaching practice in the Kings Cross Area of London I remember an angry boy flinging a chair across the room in my direction. I still have occasional nightmares about my teaching days in London. These Indian children were quite different. Many of them were under a lot of pressure from their parents to succeed. I had to teach using the Gujarat State Textbook for the appropriate Standard. The owners of the school were nice to me and I felt appreciated. The job seemed to be going well. It looked like I was to be with the school for some time. However, it soon became apparent that Fate had other plans for me.

Above: On the roof of Mrs. Bhowmik's home in Calcutta. The ladies on each side of me were both "Mrs. Ghosh" a common Bengali name. They were sweet and lovely people, open-hearted and kind.

26.

I was with The Little Flower School for about two months when I was taken ill with hepatitis. I had severe jaundice and an enlarged liver and spleen. Clearly my life was in danger. I was admitted to the Calico Mill Hospital through the kindness of Dr. Sangani, and there I received excellent treatment by experienced professionals. I was hospitalised for several weeks and received numerous visitors. Eventually it was time to return to the house at Shardar Nagar Society.

My recovery brought the offer of a less strenuous job from Mrs. Kamalini Sarabhai, who was in charge of the B.M. Institute of Mental Health in Ashram Road, Ahmedabad. Mrs. Sarabhai was a psychoanalyst, trained by Anna Freud. She asked me to call her Kamalini without the 'ben', as she explained that she was not from Gujarat. She had a jolly personality and I liked her a lot. She was the wife of Gautram Sarabhai and I found her to be an extremely caring and kind person. The Institute needed an English Language Advisor to aid the trainee doctors, psychologists and social workers to prepare their reports. Kamalini thought that I would be perfect for the position. There was a natural rapport between us and I enjoyed our association and also working with the other highly educated members of staff.

All the students at the Institute were well qualified Indians who experienced some difficulty with the English grammar.

On four afternoons a week I was also required to teach young children in the attached Gujarati medium school known as 'Balghar'. There was another school adjoining the premises. It was purely for Down's syndrome children, but apart from visiting the cheerful headmistress, Rhoda, I had no real contact with that school. I found the Gujarati children in Balghar a sheer joy to teach. I created illustrated textbooks using phonic methods. I was given a pleasant office that I shared with an elderly male teacher named Ishwarbhai. He would frequently interrupt his work to say prayers and to ring a little bell in front of a small altar. Gradually I became accustomed to this and learned to respectfully continue with my work while he chanted in his own language. Fortunately he also spoke good English and we became friends.

Meanwhile, a white lady I had befriended in the City of Ahmedabad had taken a great interest in my mediumship. Her name was Joy Saldanha. She was of Anglo-Irish extraction, and she lived with her elderly English mother in an upstairs apartment overlooking a noisy street. Their apartment was next door to the Advance Cinema. Sometimes in the evenings dramatic music and dialogue from the current movie could be heard drifting through the open balcony window. Joy had been married to an Indian Jazz pianist, and had herself been a professional singer. She had a tall, attractive biracial daughter named Carol. Through Joy I became acquainted with many of the Anglo-Indian community. They were very friendly nice people, and it was decided that we should form a psychic development circle at my house in Shardar Nagar Society. I had spoken of my experiences with the group in London and this had whetted the appetite of Joy and her friends to experience trance mediumship. We were joined by a lovely elderly lady we called 'Auntie Doris,' and a smart young schoolteacher named Gerty Robinson. Carol, Joe and Neil also sat in the circle.

Every Friday evening rickshaws bearing the different sitters for the group would arrive at the house. We managed to black out one of the small inner rooms, as we were all sitting for physical phenomena. I relaxed in a chair and soon drifted off into trance. A tape recorder was used for every session.

Several English-speaking personalities manifested, from a William Bryant who had a very deep voice to a Romanian nurse named Maria Kunz, whose voice was purely female. She described how her small village had been bombed during the First World War. She also described the beauty of her present surroundings in the spiritual realms. Several people commented, after hearing the tape recordings that if I was able to produce such diverse vocal effects under normal conditions I could easily make my living as an entertainer. Each voice had its own distinct quality and personality and appeared to be emerging from my throat while I was entranced. Interestingly, during the time we sat, no Gujarati or Hindi-speaking spirits came through. I understand that it is quite difficult for a non-English speaking spirit to influence the neural pathways of the brain of an English-speaking medium, as this would require a very deep level of control, so that was not too surprising to me. I was never quite comfortable with the idea of trance, however, as I preferred to know what was happening. The personalities that manifested were quite unlike me. Over a period of time William Bryant made some very accurate predictions and Gerty Robinson became quite attached to him. He in turn seemed to be extremely fond of her. It became something of a joke in the circle. On a more serious note, Joy's mother had developed cancer and became seriously ill. William Bryant was able to give her helpful and extremely comforting messages. Joy and her friends were always very pleasant and supportive to us, and our little group must have sat regularly for well over a year. Mr. Mohanty was also very tolerant of our sittings in the downstairs room, but he never showed any desire to join us. I think he was a little nervous of the whole thing. He did say however, that as he was passing the séance room door one Friday evening, he had stopped to listen outside and had been amazed by the clarity and individuality of the voices that he heard.

"It certainly wasn't *you* speaking," he said.

News of our experimental sittings reached the ears of a young female journalist named Suthan Kerkera. I gave her some private sittings and she began writing an article about my work in India. Her article appeared in The Sunday Standard newspaper on

November 2nd, 1975, entitled 'The Conundrum of Death.' It was a well-written article and as a result of it, I received several hundred letters from various parts of India, seeking information about my life and work. Although it took time, I did answer every letter personally. Some people were asking for books that I could not provide. Others merely wanted me to be their pen friend. It was my first experience of 'fan mail.'

During this time I also experimented with a crystal ball that had been given to me by my friend 'Remie.' One of the Calico Mill's Statisticians, a Bengali Indian named Mr. Mukherjee, once consulted me. We sat opposite each other in a semi-dark room, and I relaxed and stared into the crystal, which lay upon a black cloth. I remember telling him that he would be sponsored by an International organisation to lecture on statistics in Europe. He knew nothing about this at the time. Six months later he informed me that UNESCO had sponsored him to lecture in London and Germany. We were both quite amazed by the accuracy of this prediction and began speculating about the possibility of certain events being preordained. The whole business of 'time' is so mysterious that it has always been a major enigma. Throughout the years I have been constantly surprised by the feedback people have given me concerning my various predictions. I have absolutely no way of explaining them.

One evening at the dinner table, Mr. Mohanty told me about an amazing man who lived in South India. This man was known as Sathya Sai Baba. His followers claimed that he had performed every miracle attributed to Jesus, including raising a number of people from the dead. Each day Sathya Sai Baba would apparently materialise objects and present them as gifts to various people around him in his ashram. "In the village where he was born, he has a beautiful temple," Mr. Mohanty said, "He has also founded colleges of education and created scholarships so that poor people could have opportunities for self-improvement. Many of the chief ministers from the different states of India regularly consult him. He is very famous."

I was quite intrigued to hear this story.

"I'd like to meet that man," I said.

Mr. Mohanty smiled: "Many people have tried to see him, but have been unsuccessful. Sometimes all kinds of obstacles were put in their way. The devotees say that you can only get an audience with Baba (as they call him) if you have earned the right to do so. He is very elusive and mysterious, and he has been able to magically appear suddenly to his devotees when they have been in trouble many miles away. He preaches universal love and has all the symbols of the major world religions in his temple at Puttaparthi in South India."

"What does he look like?" I asked.

"Ah! All Western people are so concerned with appearance!" Mr. Mohanty commented.

I smiled and waited for him to continue.

"He's an Indian, but he looks like an African. He has a shock of frizzy black hair like a halo around his head and he usually wears a red or orange robe, because he is a swami or holy man. An amazing thing about him is that he regularly materialises a grey ash from the ends of his fingers. They call this mysterious ash 'vibhuti' and those who receive it either eat it or put it on their foreheads. It is said to heal many illnesses."

"Why would he give people ash?" I wondered.

"He says that everything must eventually be reduced to ashes and dust and that is the purest substance of all. He also claims to be the reincarnation of a Bombay holy man known as Shirdi Baba who lived earlier in the century. Shirdi Baba also performed miracles of healing. He would rake the fire and give some of the ash to the visitors he received each day. Using that ash blessed by the saint, many sick people were apparently cured. Sathya Sai Baba continues with that tradition."

"What a strange thing!" I said.

"Even more amazing," Mr. Mohanty continued, "is the fact that many devotees who have had a picture of Sai Baba in their homes have reported that the picture began to produce vibhuti in a very mysterious way. Investigators went to the people's homes and found nothing fraudulent, but they couldn't explain the continual appearance of the ash all around the picture."

"It sounds like the Indian equivalent of a Catholic weeping Madonna," I said.

"I thought you should know that *we* also have *our* miracles in India," Mr. Mohanty smiled, "The Christian churches think they are so superior, but we

Hindus have a great deal that we can teach *them*, if they are prepared to listen."

"I'm sure you do," I agreed, "But that Sai Baba is one holy man I really would like to meet!"

Little did I realise then that within a relatively short time my wish was to be granted.

Above: Myself and Neil with Mr. Mukherjee's family in Somnath, which is on the west coast of Gujarat State.

27.

My two years in India flew by and I enjoyed my work at the B.M. Institute. The people were cultured and friendly and treated me with respect and genuine affection. The teachers in Balghar School were particularly nice. Kamalini had a great sense of humour and I had regular meetings with her. It was like being in the presence of The Queen Mother. Kamalini was held in high esteem by the staff for her natural humanity and wisdom, and she was a true member of the Indian aristocracy. She was a wonderful lady who helped me tremendously during my final year in India. Sadly, she was later diagnosed with cancer in her shoulder bone and she informed me of this during a later visit. We talked about Laetrile and various alternative treatments for the disease. I thought Kamalini was very brave. She was a Libra and always seemed calm and balanced.

Meanwhile, Joe had decided to build a house in Ahmedabad, despite his constant complaints about the excessive heat. Mr. Mohanty warned him about the many obstacles and problems that he might have to face. I shared Mr. Mohanty's concern. Good cement was difficult to obtain. Joe was not familiar with the local rules and regulations. There was a great deal of bribery involved in getting anything done, but my determined Scorpio friend had made up his mind and no one was going to change it!

It was the summer of 1975. A plot of land was purchased in a new developing housing society that was less than a mile from where we lived. It was a flat area of the desert that had only a few isolated houses at the time. Access was down a dirt lane by the side of some fields that frequently flooded during the monsoon season.

After a blessing ceremony by a Hindu priest, building began. The contractor was a short chubby man whose crafty appearance put me on guard. He spoke good English, but his whole demeanour worried me. He was altogether too slick. Everything was "no problem" and we soon learned that those words meant quite the opposite. Eventually, when the house was near completion, a friendly neighbour pointed out that a major mistake had been made in the building of the staircase. Too few steps had been created and the outside doorway under the staircase had had to be lowered, making that area vulnerable to flooding during the rainy season. Perhaps it was a way of 'economising' on the use of cement and selling a little surplus on the black market. I never found out. Soon some ugly iron bars were added to the windows and apart from finalising a sewage connection the house was almost ready for occupation. It was at that point that the contractor decided to add an extra zero to a blank cheque that Joe had foolishly signed and handed over. The five hundred rupees owed became five thousand. When the fraud became known, Joe went berserk. He had the contractor arrested. We proceeded to the Ahmedabad police station where I watched Joe vent his rage upon the cunning little man who paced like an animal behind bars. The police seemed much amused by the whole incident and we learned the next day that the contractor had been released soon after we had left the station. No doubt he had parted with a wad of rupees in the process.

Joe then announced to Mr. Mohanty that we would be moving out of the Shardar Nagar house at the end of the month. Mr. Mohanty promptly and wisely rented a small room within easy access of the Calico Museum of Textiles, where he was employed. I was sorry to see him go, as he had been a good friend. He was a kind man and we had enjoyed many hours of conversation. Looking back, I realise now that I should also have got my own place at that time, but when you are in another country and you do not speak much of the language, you are cautious about taking such action.

The three of us did move into the newly built house. I tried to conceal the barbed wire fence around the compound by building a wall and planting trees and shrubs. Then the monsoon rains arrived and the surrounding desert flooded. Fortunately the house was built on a raised mound which somewhat protected us from the water, but mice and lizards decided to also seek refuge there from the floods. We purchased a humane mousetrap and every few days I was releasing the little critters into a dry portion of the desert. We still had no proper sewage connection and were using a temporary outhouse behind the property. We also were sleeping on mattresses placed on the floor and covered with mosquito nets. At night the ground floors became alive with a whole host of insects that moved rapidly around in the dark.

One day an elderly man named Ramanbhai from the same housing society came to our front door. He was demanding several hundred rupees in order that our sewage connection could be authorised and completed. Joe was extremely angry over this and refused to pay the money as he had already spent most of his savings on building the place. By now he was thinking that it might be good to sell this troublesome house and return to England where he had been happy for a number of years. I had talked of returning also, as I was concerned about my mother who had not been feeling too well. I could see from her frequent letters that she was concerned about me and missed me.

Joe developed violent stomach pains and was rushed into the Ahmedabad hospital where emergency treatment was performed for diverticulitis. While he was hospitalised I consulted my friend Rhoda from the B.M. Institute about ways in which to get the sewage connection completed so that the house might be put on the market. She knew the Head of the Municipal Health Department and together we sought an interview with him. He was naturally disturbed to hear of the request for 'authorisation payment' and he swiftly ordered the work team to begin the sewage connection immediately. I was very grateful to Rhoda Bilimoria for her timely aid. She was a kind and gracious lady, a Parsee with a wonderful sense of humour, and she was dedicated to educating and assisting the Down's syndrome children at the Institute.

When Joe was released from hospital he decided that we should all take a short vacation to northern India, to a hill station where the climate would be cooler and there could be temporary freedom from stress. He settled upon Mussoorie, a well-known beauty spot within eyeshot of the snow-capped Himalayas. We travelled first by train to Dehra Duhn and then caught a rather ancient bus which took us up steep, winding roads with sharp hairpin bends to the place I still consider to be next to Shangri-La in its capacity to enchant the eye and raise the spirit. The mountains were purple with salvias, and although it was November I noticed giant dahlias growing from twelve to fifteen feet high on rocky ledges. There were also apple trees and some were in blossom. I can only assume that the mild climate was confusing to them!

Mussoorie was exhilarating and intensely beautiful. We settled into a clean but rather Spartan hotel and from there began exploring this famous hill station. Tibetan refugees had made their home in the nearby 'Happy Valley.' We paid a visit to the Tibetan school and I had the experience of turning the enormous prayer wheels and seeing the beautiful examples of Tibetan art and culture. Since watching the Ronald Colman version of 'Lost Horizon' I had always been fascinated by this part of the world. Maybe I hoped to find the magic doorway through to other dimensions where I might meet Babaji and other spiritual teachers mentioned in the writings of Paramahansa Yogananda. In any case, I was totally captivated by what I saw at this amazing place.

Back in Ahmedabad, Joe sold the house to a bank manager at quite a low price. We all began making arrangements to return to England. My mother was extremely happy and offered to let us stay at her house in Huntingdon until we found our own accommodation. Joe had no problem returning to the United Kingdom, as he had become a British subject some years earlier and The British High Commission in Bombay stamped Neil's Indian passport with an Entry Certificate, as Neil could successfully prove that his brother was his legal guardian. We made one more trip to Calcutta to see Mrs. Bhowmik and her family, then flew to New Delhi and from there on to London Heathrow. It was February 1976, and I had been in India for just over two very exciting and educational years. I would never forget the many wonderful friends I had made and the kindness and hospitality of the Indian people.

28.

Back in England the three of us moved in with my parents. They were overjoyed that I was home from Asia. I applied for work as a teacher in the Huntingdon area and within a few days a pleasant round-faced man from the education department rang my mother's doorbell. I still believe this was some kind of Divine intervention, seeking to reassure me that my services were very much needed in my hometown. The energetic man was John Baguley, senior advisory remedial teacher for the area. He wanted me on his team of peripatetic teachers. John and I had an immediate rapport and I admired his wonderfully inventive teaching aids. He liked the phonic methods I had used in India and I was interviewed and accepted. John was a very gifted and supportive man, who radiated warmth and vitality that was quite exceptional. We are still friends to this day.

Soon my mother found the extra cooking more than she could handle, and within a few weeks I bought a three-bedroom mobile home in a village outside Huntingdon. A small car was purchased and I was able to visit the local schools to help the children with their reading. I was also sent to St. Ives to assist a number of Indian and Pakistani immigrant children. My knowledge of the culture was quite valuable and the students responded to me with warmth and friendliness.

Joe and Neil stayed with me at the mobile home for a short time, but as our living conditions were rather cramped, Joe sought to rent a house from the local council. Later, for employment reasons, they both moved back to London and Joe found a very sweet Bengali girl from Calcutta and was married. Sometime later, Neil also met his future wife Susan and they both returned to her native Australia.

Meanwhile I once again became involved with the activities of the Huntingdon Spiritualist Church. I joined the band of excellent healers and took some of the church services. One day I spoke of the miracles of Sathya Sai Baba in India. My friends Bob and Ann Copley were seated in the congregation. Afterwards, Bob came up to me and said: "Brian I have to meet that man. If you take me to India I will pay your fare!"

What an opportunity!

Bob had been in correspondence with The Divine Power Research and Service Society in Bombay. The President was Brigadier Dr. K.K. Datey. He had studied medicine in Edinburgh and had strings of letters after his name. He had also been the cardiologist to India's former President. Dr. Datey expressed the desire for Bob and I to do some lectures and demonstrations for the members of his society upon our arrival in Bombay. Bob immediately accepted, but Ann fearfully turned down the invitation to accompany us. "India frightens me," she said, "There's just so much poverty!" Bob respected his wife's feelings and she remained at home.

In July 1977, the two of us flew to Bombay and were greeted by new friends at Santa Cruz airport. I had written to my friend Joy Saldanha in Ahmedabad and she also made a trip to see us. It was quite an emotional reunion. A pleasant room had been reserved for Bob and I at the Taj luxury hotel. We were guests of the Society.

Bob had brought a large reel of 8mm coloured film of his trip to Manila in the Philippines where he had studied the remarkable abilities of native healers to perform something known as 'psychic surgery.' Dr. Datey had plans to bring some of these healers to India where he hoped they might be able to not only heal the sick, but to teach their extraordinary skills to suitable candidates.

In 'psychic surgery' it appears that the healers have the ability to diagnose the problem area of the body, to place their hands over the spot, and then to slide their fingertips into the mysteriously separated flesh and to pull out diseased tissues. On the face of it this sounds like a wonderful fairy tale, yet Bob had a unique reel of film that showed in close-up the whole extraordinary procedure. Trickery cannot explain the instant removal of large tumours and goitres. People, who had been suffering one moment, were completely free of their disorder after the psychic surgeons had worked on them! Clearly this is uncharted territory and the healers are not following known physical laws. In the Philippines the Christian Spiritualist Movement was the umbrella organisation for much of this activity, and people from many parts of the world were seeking these unorthodox methods of treatment. Harold Sherman first drew public attention to this in his amazing book entitled *Wonder Healers of the Philippines*, which contains explicit photographs of psychic surgery. Dr. Datey had also witnessed this form of treatment, so he was open to its possibility.

In Bombay Dr. Datey, a short, slim, dapper man in a pinstriped suit and bow tie had organised an intensive round of lectures, demonstrations and film shows to keep us busy. Many doctors from the local hospitals attended the showing of Bob's incredible film. At one point in the film a psychic surgeon was shown removing an eyeball, dipping the eye in a bowl of water and then replacing the eye in the hollow socket. Whatever happened to the optic nerve in the process remains a complete mystery, and the patient certainly did not have a glass eye but reported perfect vision afterwards. Such events stretch one's belief system to breaking point. Whatever is happening here? Will it ever be possible for conventional science to explain such things?

In the meantime, I was called upon to do several demonstrations of mental mediumship in the Birla Theatre. Conditions were far from ideal. The stage lights were very bright and I had difficulty seeing the several hundred members of the audience as I stood in front of the microphone. No assistant was there to carry a portable mike from one message-recipient to another. Indeed a second microphone was just not available. The responses to my messages in that large theatre were at times unclear, and I found the whole procedure quite stressful. In spite of that I did succeed in giving several messages that were accepted and understood. The Indian names are not easy to transmit as one can imagine. The audience however seemed fascinated by what I was doing, and at the end of each demonstration people rushed forward to the stage, climbed on it and I was garlanded with flowers. Several people tried to touch my feet, which I found somewhat embarrassing, as I was not pretending to be any kind of mystical guru.

Minaz Merchant of *The Times of India* attended one of my demonstrations as a sceptic and consequently wrote a rather condescending article. He obviously had little understanding of the difficulties involved in spirit communication. We had earlier attended a buffet given in our honour at the newspaper, where I had met Mr. Kushwant Singh the Editor. It was known later that Singh had visited Sathya Sai Baba as a non-believer and the holy man had apparently materialised a bottle of whiskey for the delighted newspaperman. Sai Baba also stroked Singh's beard and created a powerful perfume that Singh was unable to wash away for quite some time. This was reported in an interview with Kushwant Singh that was later broadcast by the BBC.

At the Birla Theatre a number of people said afterwards that they were quite surprised that their deceased family members were still in the spirit world as they assumed those loved ones had reincarnated. I had to explain that reincarnation was true but not for everybody and not immediately. We might have a 'summer vacation' of several hundred years in the astral world before returning to the earthly schoolroom, and many people might just move on to a higher level of the astral rather than return to this contaminating planet called Earth. There were many variables operating and exactly how it worked was known only to God.

After my final demonstration of clairvoyance and clairaudience and Bob's showing of his film, we left the theatre surrounded by an enormous crowd. We were about to climb in the back of Dr. Datey's car when a number of crippled and afflicted people pushed forward from the street and asked for Bob's help and healing. He told me afterwards that he felt a deep sense of impotency and humility at the sheer demand for his services. It saddened him deeply to feel that he could do nothing for those people at that time. We took our seats in the car and I was about to close the door when suddenly an elderly beggar dressed in rags startled me by his appearance at my side. He leaned into the car and said in perfect English. *"You will visit Sai Baba and he will give you vibhuti like this..."* The mysterious beggar then poured a white ash from his fingers directly into my hand. The ash spilled on my clothes and I was so astonished I did not know what to say. I recoiled somewhat in shock that an old man in such tattered garments should know that Bob and I were to visit Sathya Sai Baba in south India. Even if there had been gossip in the streets, the people could not have had knowledge of our intended journey. It was very weird indeed!

Later, in Dr. Datey's surgery Bob Copley at 75 years of age was presented with the supreme challenge of attempting to relieve almost a hundred different health conditions. Many of the celebrities of Bombay were there. Bob was not a psychic surgeon but a magnetic healer. Dr. Datey and his team carefully monitored each patient while I observed the extraordinary results.

Apprehensively, I watched Bob kneel down beside a bed on which lay a young man that had severe curvature of the spinal cord. It looked like a serious condition. Bob placed his large hands on the man's bare back and the treatment began. Within a few minutes it became obvious that the back was gradually straightening under pressure and the patient appeared to be feeling no pain. Soon, he got up and walked away joyfully in an upright position.

A deaf and dumb boy was brought to Bob for treatment and with the aid of a Gujarati-speaking interpreter, the boy was induced to speak numbers first in his own language and then in English. His parents said that his speech had merely consisted of unintelligible sounds until that day at the clinic. It appeared that there was significant improvement in the boy's hearing, enabling him to understand the instructions given to him.

As the day went on, Dr. Datey noted that Bob's heartbeat was accelerating rapidly during the treatments, and at one point he was concerned for Bob's physical safety and almost called a halt to the proceedings. Fortunately Bob was a strong man and the people were tremendously enthusiastic and supportive after the first few successes!

Later, we both had our brainwave patterns tested on the electroencephalograph and Dr. Datey carefully monitored my heartbeat and different responses. The few days that we spent working at his clinic were most productive and he was a kind and supportive man. I had never before conducted a demonstration of mediumship in a doctor's office. I actually did this while Bob was working in the next room!

"If this can help my patients then that's what I'm concerned about!" Dr. Datey said, realistically.

During this Bombay visit Mr. & Mrs. Kartikey Mahadevia kindly invited us for a few days as guests in their apartment. He was a businessman who was doing research into the wheat grass therapy and into various agricultural improvements that could help better feed India. He was kind enough to drive me to a Gova Gas Plant where we inspected the facilities and learned how ordinary cow dung could be converted into useful household gas for cooking and heating. So abundant was the supply of this natural gas that lamps and burners were kept operating 24 hours in order to avoid excessive build-up of pressure in the large cylinders.

One day, while descending the stairs outside Kartikey's apartment I saw this thin, grey-haired American lady approaching me. We greeted each other curiously, and I discovered from her energetic conversation that she was Dr. Anne Wigmore, a

238

specialist in natural healing and wheat grass therapy. She was the celebrated author of *"Be Your Own Doctor"* and she had founded the Hippocrates Health Institute in Boston, Massachusetts. When she knew who I was, she asked me very directly for 'a reading'. Unfortunately there was no time to fit this in as we were due to leave by train for Bangalore to visit Whitefields, where Sathya Sai Baba spent a great deal of his time. We had no guarantee that Baba would be in residence there, as he frequently visited temples and other holy places around India, so our journey was a complete act of faith. The tickets were purchased, we said emotional goodbyes to the kind Mahadevia family, Kartikey drove us to the station and we climbed on the long, crowded Bangalore train to begin the next part of our incredible adventure.

Above: July, 1977. This photo was taken in the consulting room with Brigadier Dr. K.K. Datey and Bob Copley. Dr. Datey had studied in Scotland, U.K. and was a highly qualified cardiologist to one of India's former Presidents.

29.

I had suggested to Bob that travelling by train was the best way to see something of the Indian countryside, and he had agreed. As we took our seats in the first class compartment, however, I could see that he was exhausted and obviously feeling unwell.

"My stomach feels so weird," he said.

"Did you drink any unboiled water?" I queried.

"I drank a lot of water at the clinic," Bob said, "The maidservant brought it to me, and I assumed it was from the boiled supply that Dr. Datey had provided. Uh – uh! I have to get to the bathroom quickly!"

And my tall, bald-headed friend made a speedy exit down the corridor. How well I knew his condition!

The journey to Bangalore was extremely uncomfortable for Bob. I gave him some medication I had for diarrhoea and reflected upon the power of the e.coli organism. Whatever miracles God may have allowed at the clinic, I prayed for a further one on the train!

After an exhausting journey lasting many hours, we finally reached Bangalore. We reserved two bunk beds in a communal retiring room and there we were fortunate enough to overhear some Baba devotees discussing the famous holy man. We were in luck! He was at Whitefields, a mere half-hour journey from town.

Next morning a taxi took us at hair-raising speed across Bangalore and out into dry, sandy countryside. The taxi halted outside a decorated gate in a large, walled compound. Facing us inside was the impressive boys' hostel built by Baba from donations. It was beautifully bright and colourful! To the right hand side of the hostel in a separate compound was the private house Baba used. He lived quite simply, occupying only one room. He had dedicated himself to improving educational facilities in India. He claimed to be sent by God as a spiritual messenger to help transform the world. No accommodation was available for us at the hostel, but by talking to a number of local people we were able to rent a small room in an unfinished house behind the main building.

Sadly, Bob's stomach condition had not improved. A pharmacy was located and medicine obtained. Bob was feeling quite weak and ill. I boiled all water and cooked for him on a small Primus stove that I had wisely taken with me. We slept on simple mattresses on the floor. We had no mosquito nets but I burned the coils which somewhat deterred the humming insects.

Next morning we made our way to the Boys' Hostel. Many people were gathered in the compound. Some were seated beneath the shade of trees and watched us curiously as we passed. Bob found a shady spot to recline and I walked a little further into the grounds. Suddenly I spotted Baba in his bright red robe. He was standing silently near the edge of the trees. He was not very tall, yet he had an impressive appearance with his black halo of African-type hair. Suddenly he turned and looked straight into my eyes. I had the most peculiar tingling sensation throughout my spine. I stared back at him for a moment but could not bring myself to approach him, as I was not sure of the protocol involved. Many thoughts raced through my mind. I wondered whether he was really a Divine being. He looked so small and human and yet the eyes had a brilliant, hypnotic quality that was most remarkable. They seemed like dark pools of infinite knowledge. I felt that Baba was examining me carefully for those few seconds in which his shining eyes caught mine. I was literally frozen in my tracks and waited for further development, a sign that it was acceptable to approach him. However, he turned his head in the direction of some devotees who sat nearby and walked slowly away. I felt somewhat relieved, as I was still deeply awed by his magical presence and perhaps in some way felt myself unworthy of his attention.

I returned to Bob who was resting beneath the tree. By now we could both see Baba at some distance moving among the people. The morning sun was beating down and the heat gradually became oppressive. Soon we returned to the small rented house and I prepared a simple meal.

"Baba didn't come anywhere near me," Bob complained, "And I've travelled such a long way."

I felt quite sorry for him. He seemed so desperate to meet Baba.

"Perhaps I'm sick now because I have to purge away some of my sins," he stated mournfully.

"Oh no!" I reassured him.

"When I was a young man I did some things I shouldn't have done," Bob continued, "My hands weren't always clean. They say that Baba knows everything about us."

"I'm sure he allows for the fact that we're human," I said, "I'm not perfect but he did take a look at me, so just be patient."

"You have no idea..." Bob mumbled.

Whatever private regrets he may have had, I felt it was not my business to enquire further. We do judge ourselves when we pass over, but many begin the process much earlier. I thought it wise to distract him with other conversation.

The sun set quite early. As there was no electricity installed in the unfinished building we lit some candles and Bob rested on his mattress. I took a walk in the surrounding fields and was approached by a small boy with shining dark eyes who began fearlessly questioning me. He must have been about eleven years of age, but his command of English was surprising:

"Where you from, Sahib?"

"From England"

"Is that cold place?"

"It can be," I smiled.

"My brother sick. Need to see doctor. Can you help?"

"What's wrong with your brother?" I asked.

"Fever. Need money for injection."

"How much?"

"Ten rupees," he said, hopefully. Then while waiting for my reply he took my hand and asked me to sit down. There were no seats available so we both sat cross-legged on the ground observing each other. He was a cute child and may have been lying to get money. I wasn't sure. He stretched out his small brown hand and looked at me with pleading eyes. I hadn't the heart to refuse this direct request and found two five-rupee bills in my pocket. I handed them over. He smiled with a perfect set of teeth and came closer to me, patting my leg.

"Sahib good man."

"Do you go to school?" I asked.

"In village," he replied.

"I am here to see Sai Baba," I said, "But my friend is sick. He is resting."

"Oh, sorry friend sick. You in that house?" he asked, pointing to our unfinished hovel.

"Not for long," I said.

"You go tomorrow?"

"I don't know," I replied.

We talked for some time about his family and his life in the village. He was quite the conversationalist! Soon it was time to leave and the boy walked slowly back across the field, waving goodbye to this fair-skinned stranger from another country. Such is the friendliness of India.

Bob was sleeping when I returned. I had forgotten to light mosquito coils and upon waking he complained that he had been bitten on his face and on his bald head. The coils being lit, fragrant incense filling the air, we both settled down for a tropical night of continuous clicking noises of insects, punctuated by the croak of frogs from the ditch behind the house.

Next morning Bob felt too weak to accompany me to the hostel. The medication had brought his bowels a little under control, but the side effects were devastating.

"I can't leave you here alone," I protested, "I think we should get a taxi and find a hotel in town."

"You go and see Baba," Bob insisted, "I'll be all right."

He was not one to argue with, so I walked down the dirt lane to the Boys' Hostel and entered the gate. A small crowd was already assembled, ladies in one area, gentlemen in another and all seated cross-legged on individual mats or blankets on the sandy earth. I joined the other men and sat down as the familiar orange-robed figure emerged from the house. The crowd's emotions seemed to surge through me as I stared at Baba walking gracefully towards us. He made curious little circular movements in the air with his right hand as he approached where I sat. With my 8mm cine camera I filmed and photographed him at close range. He spoke to people in the crowd and accepted letters from them, which he later passed to an elderly gentleman assisting him. He seldom smiled but his black eyes burned with an intensity that suggested tremendous mental activity. People scooped up the sand where he had walked; others touched his feet as he passed, but he discouraged the outstretched hands from continuing to do that. In one place a carpet of flowers had been reverently laid for him to walk upon. He stopped to touch various devotees and to bestow blessings. One lady garlanded him with flowers. Soon he appeared to be materialising small objects that he gave to several individuals, but I was too far away to clearly observe the exact procedure.

A number of people were called for private interviews. They included a young Sikh post office worker from Singapore who, I later learned, was going blind. When the chosen few had disappeared into the house I got into conversation with a group of clean-looking young men from the Sathya Sai Arts and Commerce College. They told me that Baba would be attending the annual prize-giving there on the following afternoon, but admission was by ticket only. They told me that they enjoyed being students at the college but they were expected to work hard and obtain good marks in their exams. Competition for employment in India was intensely fierce and there was much pressure from their families to succeed. Nevertheless they seemed happy, well-adjusted young men who knew nothing of drugs or alcohol abuse or any of the other plagues of Western society. There was a clean-cut physical beauty about them that was most impressive.

After purchasing some items of food from a small shop outside the compound, I returned to Bob who was madly scratching his insect bites.

"Did you see Baba and ask him about me?"

"He didn't come close enough," I said, "But he was accepting letters from different people, so maybe if I write him a note and have it ready tomorrow morning he will take it from me."

"Yes, do that," Bob agreed, "I've come such a long way. I must see him."

On the morning of July 30th, 1977, as I entered the compound and approached the seated crowd, an elderly silver-haired man with glasses spoke to me.

"I saw you here yesterday," he said, "and I will be honoured if you will take my place over there on the front row."

It would have been ungracious to refuse such a kind offer. Smiling, I thanked him. Then stepping around the people, I managed to seat myself on his small rush mat, holding the letter I had written to Baba requesting an interview and some guidance on Bob's illness. The young Sikh postal worker who had been called for an interview the previous morning sat near to me:

"Baba is God!" he enthused, nodding his turbaned head; "Yesterday Baba materialised vibhuti for me and put some on my face. He stroked my eyes and told me I would get my sight back. Already I can see more clearly. I feel great emotional relief because my job depends upon my eyes. If I am without sight I cannot work."

"I understand how you feel," I said, "I have a sick elderly man with me and I am concerned about his health also."

"Baba will surely help you," the Sikh replied.

We settled down to await Baba's appearance while some of the devotees began singing Indian bhajans (religious songs). Bathed in brilliant sunlight, the white shirts of the men radiated an ethereal otherworldly quality. The peace, the love and the harmony within that crowd was something one felt at a deep level, enabling contact with a blissful state of consciousness that seemed timeless and eternal.

Baba suddenly appeared in the gateway of the house and there was a murmur from the crowd. Many hands reached out for a blessing. Baba took a small slate and wrote on it, handing the slate to a young woman. I waited apprehensively on the front row, the letter in my hand. Next moment, Baba turned and looked straight at me. I felt an indescribable thrill, a tingling in the back and on the top of the head. He approached me swiftly and took my letter, handing it to the elderly man who accompanied him. Then turning my right palm uppermost he immediately materialised vibhuti from his fingertips. I stared at the mysterious grey substance pouring from the ends of his brown fingers. It was all over in a few seconds, and my palm was filled with the fragrant holy ash for which he was famous. I was overwhelmed by the experience.

"Thank you, Baba," I said.

"All right," he replied.

"Bless you," I said.

"Thank you," he responded.

He walked on and spoke to others. I put some of the ash on my tongue. It had a slightly sweet taste. I put some on my forehead. Then a number of brown hands reached out to take it from me. I allowed several men to dip into my palm, to take a pinch and smear the sacred ash upon their own foreheads. It meant so much to them. A moment later I was gently rebuked by one of the elderly male assistants dressed in white.

"Baba has given his special blessing to you. The vibhuti is for you only."

Reluctantly I closed my palm, feeling uncomfortable to refuse the surrounding people something they regarded as very precious. I didn't quite understand the meaning of it all, or what I was supposed to do with it, but I had certainly seen the magical appearance of the ash in brilliant sunlight. There was no trickery. Baba's hand had made actual contact with my palm while the grey substance oozed from his fingers. It was a unique and memorable experience!

Elated by the blessing I had received, I watched Baba move gracefully among the crowd. He was certainly a unique phenomenon. He leaned forward and spoke briefly to a lady who sat quite close to the men's area. Then I saw the familiar circular movements of his hand in the air and a beautiful necklace studded with glittering green stones seemed to fall from his palm into the lady's hand. Her joy was immeasurable. Her face shone like the sun. She had received a beautiful gift of jewellery brought from…another dimension, another space-time continuum? There was certainly no place in the flimsy orange robe for him to conceal such objects and the accusation by sceptics that he was merely a clever magician just did not hold water. He had literally snatched those objects that he materialised out of the air. What an extraordinary gift! I had seen it, I had experienced it, and there was no way I could continue to disbelieve it!

When Baba finished selecting the people he wished to 'interview' and disappeared into the house, I made my way, with closed palm holding what was left of the precious vibhuti, to tell Bob about these extraordinary events. One thing comforted me: I had been able to give Baba my personal letter. Now we would wait to see what should be done.

30.

Bob lay patiently on his mattress on the floor, scratching his mosquito bites and sipping boiled water from a plastic bottle. Sadly, when I opened my palm there was little left of the grey vibhuti. He listened to my account of the astonishing events, then said wearily:

"I feel so ill. I feel like I'm going to die. Baba doesn't want to see me! I know that!"

I told Bob about the prize giving to take place at the college that afternoon and reassured him that Baba already had my letter asking for help.

"Don't give up hope," I said, "At least you're keeping food down and you're resting."

Bob looked sadly up at me:

"I wish I had your youth and strength. I'd give anything to be young again."

"Look at the wonderful results you had while helping those sick people in Bombay," I reminded him, "God won't abandon you, Bob. Believe me."

"I hope not," he sighed.

Again I prepared a simple meal on the Primus stove and was relieved to see that Bob appeared to enjoy it. After eating, he seemed a little stronger:

"Go back to the College," he said, "and try to get a message from Baba for me, will you?"

As reluctant as I was to leave him alone, I could not deny his request.

That afternoon many people gathered in the compound of the Sathya Sai Arts and Commerce College. A public address system had been installed.

I heard from the people gossiping around me that Chief Ministers and many celebrities were to be present. I stood at the front of the crowd waiting for Baba to arrive. My cine camera was ready for action. The college was beautifully decorated for the event and I began speaking to a woman whose son was a student.

"I am so proud of my boy," she told me, "He has learned spiritual values and has a good foundation to his life. Baba has turned him into a wonderful human being!"

Her enthusiasm was totally sincere.

The large crowd waited patiently in the hot sun. I spoke again to the young Sikh postal worker from Singapore.

"My eyes continue to get stronger," he said, brightly.

"Well, you recognised me!" I said, jokingly.

Of course he did! I was the only white man in that crowd of faithful Indians!

Shortly after this, a large white chauffeur-driven car pulled up in front of me and the orange-robed figure emerged. I was thrilled by what followed. Instead of entering the building, Baba walked around the car, faced where I was filming and raised his right hand. One felt the intake of breath of the people nearby. I felt it was Baba's gesture of acknowledgement. Then he went quickly into the building.

After he had gone, I spoke to an elderly man who was directing ticket holders inside. I explained about Bob's weak condition and my natural concern for his well-being. I asked directly whether Baba could help us. To my surprise the man asked me to wait and said that he would consult Baba on the matter. I could hardly believe my ears. I had begun to feel quite desperate, as we were both far from home. Bob was no longer a young man and the initial elation of his success in Bombay was fast vanishing. He was literally fighting for his life, believing that he was being punished for past wrongdoing.

After about ten minutes the elderly man emerged from the college and said: "Baba wants you to take your friend to the Ashoka hotel in Bangalore. Baba will be going to Puttaparthi on Monday. You may both go there when your friend recovers."

Much relieved, I thanked the man who obviously had access to Baba that was denied to most of us. After recording some of the prize-giving speech that came through the loudspeaker, I hurried back to tell Bob that Baba had requested our immediate removal to the Ashoka hotel. You can imagine his excitement at the news, and the extraordinary thing is that no sooner had I conveyed that message than a small boy appeared at the open doorway of the house and asked whether we would like him to get a taxi for us. "Please!" we chorused, and Bob looked really happy for the first time in several days.

I packed the stove and cooking utensils. Bob suddenly acquired the energy to push his clothes into a canvas bag and the taxi arrived just at the right moment. Within forty-five minutes we had booked in at the Ashoka hotel and were taken to a comfortable room with twin beds, a pleasant bathroom with hot running water and all the Western facilities that we had missed.

After showering and changing Bob reported a distinct improvement in his energy. We went down to the dining room for an evening meal and were greeted by a pleasant Sikh waiter who looked at Bob and said: "I see you have been very ill, Sahib. Let me take care of you."

We told the Sikh waiter about our visit to Whitefields and that Sathya Sai Baba had instructed us to move to that hotel.

"I am a Baba devotee," he informed us, "I will be happy to serve you."

And what wonderful service he gave! He took much trouble in explaining the different items on the menu, and he recommended that Bob eat a light meal that evening because of his sensitive stomach. Fortunately, I had a good appetite and had remained healthy, so I was able to enjoy a delicious Indian vegetarian meal that was beautifully prepared and served. Good Indian vegetarian food takes a lot of beating!

That night Bob slept almost naked under the ceiling fan and when we awoke the next morning he surprised me by asking me to look carefully at the insect bites he had had on his body.

"I can hardly feel them," he said.

The itching had gone, and as he sat up in his underwear it was obvious to me that the numerous mosquito bites on his shoulders, back, legs and thighs, as well as those on his bald head were almost completely healed! I was highly delighted for him and not surprised when he said emphatically:

"Baba has cured me! I know it!"

When we went down for breakfast the kind Sikh waiter greeted us with a smile. Looking at Bob he commented:

"I can see you are much improved, Sahib. I think you should have papaya for breakfast because that will heal your sensitive stomach."

So Bob had papaya and I had an omelette.

We had just finished eating and were leaving the dining room when a young American named Steve greeted us, probably because we were the only visible Westerners.

"Hi," he said, "Did you know that the Dalai Lama's upstairs?"

Bob's face lit up. Some years earlier he had helped raise money for a meditation centre in Scotland to house some of the Tibetan monks who had fled from their country after the Chinese invasion.

"Wonderful!" Bob exclaimed, "I've always wanted to meet him!"

We chatted with Steve for a few minutes and then proceeded upstairs to a large conference room where several hundred Tibetan people were gathered for The Dalai Lama to address them. While I watched from the back, Bob strode fearlessly down the central aisle and put his hands together in greeting to the Dalai Lama, while shouting out the name "Trumpa. Scotland."

His Holiness appeared to recognise the reference and smiled broadly. There was a brief exchange between them. Bob then bowed respectfully and returned to me at the back of the room.

"Baba must have known about this," he said, excitedly, "What a great opportunity to pay my respects to his Holiness!"

Bob was as pleased as Punch! I thanked The Great Designer upstairs for restoring my friend's good humour.

After two days at the Ashoka Hotel we went by taxi to Baba's birthplace of Puttaparthi, a hundred and thirty miles north of Bangalore. The latter part of the journey was through desolate country, dotted with date palms and cacti. In several places the road had been washed away by former monsoon floods. At one point the taxi juddered over mud honeycombed by the feet of cattle. A bus and several other vehicles passed us on a narrow upland track where huge blocks of stone bulged from the dusty earth.

"This is the journey that Baba frequently makes," I thought.

There seemed to be a parallel with Jesus going through the wilderness, a deliberate shunning of material comforts, a testing of one's tenacity of purpose and willingness to put aside all outward show of affluence.

Over the meandering road through the wilderness our taxi jolted on until we began to descend to a green and fertile valley, to the village of Puttaparthi, where Sathya Sai Baba, 'the Christ of India', had his headquarters. Here, I reflected, could be the beginning of the transformation of one's basic nature, resulting from a sudden illumination, an awareness of the divine. Now, there was no turning back, and only anticipation of what lay ahead, and some surprising events were in store for us as we approached a high wall and the entrance to *Prasanti Nilayam*, Baba's abode of peace.

Above: The enormous crowd At Whitefields, Bangalore. Baba regularly demonstrated his powers of materialization of precious gems and vibhuti.

31.

I noticed several buses lined up outside the compound wall as we drove through the gateway and were taken to the central accommodation office. There, our driver was informed that he must first take us to the Police Station where all foreign passports had to be checked and recorded, before their owners would be allowed into the compound.

After a short drive up the dusty road to a small whitewashed building we had a brief chat with a friendly policeman in shorts, signed a large book, and were then driven back to the central accommodation office.

Devotees of Baba had erected large blocks of flats in the compound. Some were still under construction at the time. When the devotees were not in residence they allowed visiting pilgrims to rent these individual flats for a modest fee of five rupees a day. The office allocated us a first floor room with a western-type toilet. The room was completely bare. One tap supplied water for only a few hours in the morning and again late in the evening. There was mosquito netting over the barred window and a laundry service and sweepers were available. We had only sleeping bags and inflatable mattresses and a tiny Primus stove to prepare the simplest of meals. It was a Spartan existence.

Later we explored the compound. Near the office a notice drew visitors' attention to Baba's disapproval of alcohol, drugs and immodest behaviour. I made a mental note that I must not take a sip from the half bottle of brandy I had brought with me from Bombay. Visitors were also requested to conduct themselves in a quiet and respectful manner. No problem in that area, I thought. Nearby was a canteen that served highly spiced vegetarian food, but men and women had to eat in segregated areas. We tried the canteen but were not impressed by the menu. It was way too spicy for Bob's delicate stomach.

We soon found our way to Baba's beautiful temple, which was quite unlike any other I had seen in India. It has three domes, is ornate without being fussy, and is coloured an attractive pastel yellow and sky blue. Baba gives his thousands of private interviews in a room at the side of the temple. During daily *darshan* (blessings) he walks among the crowd and chooses certain people for interview. One cannot book a 'sitting' with him. Many have sought interviews and he has passed them by. Baba's criteria for selection are quite mysterious, but nearly all those chosen have serious problems or are actively involved in spiritual work. We learned that Baba dislikes being touched unless he initiates the contact. He also refuses to accept money for himself.

Bob and I waited cross-legged on the sand outside the temple for the afternoon *darshan*. There were fewer people here than at Whitefields, though on occasions such as Baba's birthday celebration on November 23rd, 1975, the crowd was so enormous that he gave his blessing from the air – in a helicopter!

Eventually Baba appeared. I filmed and photographed him. He glanced briefly at me but passed by. I felt some disappointment, but remembered reading of his unpredictability. At Whitefields he had accepted my letter in which I requested a personal interview, and he had given me vibhuti, the "holy ash." Surely that was enough! Unlike many people around me I had no serious problem and was in good health on this trip to India. After Baba had chosen the people who would be interviewed he disappeared into his private room. A queue began to form outside the temple for the hourly meeting. Bob and I joined the line anxiously anticipating our first sight of the interior of this beautiful building. Barefoot we entered, ladies on the left and gentlemen on the right. The whole building had a spacious interior with numerous openings near the roof for natural light to enter. To the rear of the temple was a life-sized model of the blue-faced god Krishna, riding with the warrior Arjuna in his chariot. The whole model was beautifully coloured, illuminated and carefully roped off.

Bob sat with his back against a nearby pillar for support. He was experiencing the difficulty that most westerners have in sitting cross-legged for long periods. On both sides of the temple were paintings representing scenes from the Hindu scriptures. Small birds twittered and flew about under the ornamental ceiling. At the front left hand side of the temple facing us sat a life-sized figure of an elderly man, the original Sai Baba of Shirdi from Bombay. Sai Baba died in 1918 and told his devotees he would reincarnate in eight years in South India in a completely different body. The present Sathya Sai Baba claims to be Shirdi Baba reborn.

Behind the 'waxwork' model was a full-length painting framed in shining silver of the elderly, bearded Bombay saint who also had many devotees during his earth life. Shirdi Baba would frequently give some of the ash from his fire to sick people. Many miracles were reported in his time. Sathya Sai Baba's vibhuti represents a link with his former incarnation as well as a possible reminder that all things in the material world must return to ashes and dust, and that the spiritual reality is the only lasting one.

To the right of Shirdi Baba's picture was a familiar one of Swami in his orange robe, also framed in silver. Just in front of that picture to the right was an empty throne. It would obviously be occupied at some time during the singing by Baba.

The temple bells began jingling. A singer at the front led the congregation in many different *bhajans* (religious songs). The people followed, some swaying hypnotically to the rhythms. The surrounding atmosphere seemed incredibly clear and pure. I felt a tingling in my back and spine and a cool sensation on the top of my head. I could not understand the words of the hymns, but I sensed their sweetness and beauty and their essential Indian quality. I lost all sense of time in that temple. I felt transported to another dimension of reality. It was quite an emotional experience, yet at the same time my mind felt supremely clear.

Halfway through the singing Baba suddenly entered the temple and sat on the empty throne. The people's voices thrilled with renewed energy as he raised his right hand and began gently beating time to the music. As I gazed transfixed at Baba I saw a brilliant series of lights around his head. There seemed to be several colours, including green, extending from the shock of frizzy hair. I felt instinctively, "This man is another Christ." Any doubts I had had regarding him dispersed. I felt a willing participant in his charismatic presence. This was the effect that Baba had on most people. One could not ignore his sheer spiritual existence, his radiant energy. He was utterly unique!

During the next few days Bob and I attended the *darshans* regularly and spoke to many people who had been interviewed by Baba. No word of criticism was ever spoken of him. A young man showed me a beautiful gold ring that Baba had materialised and given him as a present. On the ring was a small, embossed image of Baba's head. I touched the ring and admired its beauty.

"Baba gives many things to people each day," the man said, "He hopes that by giving us the things *we* want, we will eventually learn to want the things *he* wants for us."

"What are those things?" I asked.

"We need freedom from the materialistic world, to be transformed into loving and spiritual beings and to become like Baba, full of bliss."

"Do you think Baba is God?" I asked.

"Baba has complete knowledge of all of us," he replied, "and still loves us. In that way he is like God. You could not have come here to Prasanti Nilayam unless Baba allowed it. Many people have tried. All kinds of obstacles have been put in their path. You are here only by Baba's grace."

I found his words difficult to accept, but they served to underline his intense devotion to and belief in Baba.

The next day during *bhajan* singing in the temple a small, elderly man came and sat beside me. He appeared to be in a state of great excitement and exhilaration. He leaned over and whispered confidentially to me: "I've just seen Baba. He has solved all my problems! He is wonderful!"

"What did he do?" I asked in a whisper.

"So many things!" the man enthused, "A man from Bombay went after me. I watched Baba put his hand straight into the man's body and take out a cancer. Baba operated. The sick man was healed immediately! Baba is God!"

This tiny gentleman with the cloth bag on his shoulder was a perfect stranger. He had no knowledge of the films of psychic surgery Bob and I had been showing to large audiences in Bombay. I watched tears run down this little man's cheeks as the occupants of the temple sang beautifully around us. Having heard so much from many people regarding Baba's great powers of healing, I did not doubt the man's words. He was obviously overcome by awe at what he had seen. His system was in some kind of spiritual shock! I put my arm around his shoulders and hugged him. He opened a small bag and showed me several tiny folded packets of *vibhuti* Baba had materialised for him. On each packet was a picture of Baba and a blessing printed in Telegu script (Baba's language). To my great delight the man gave me one of the small packets, which I eventually brought back to England and gave to a woman friend who was crippled with rheumatoid arthritis.

Our whispered conversation during the singing attracted disapproving looks from a rather haughty-faced woman nearby, so we desisted from further exchange. When the meeting was finished, the little man carrying his cloth shoulder bag of precious vibhuti waved to me and disappeared among the crowd. So now I knew that Baba himself could perform psychic surgery. That was the supreme act of healing. I found myself unconsciously wishing that I could witness such extraordinary things under circumstances where there could not possibly be any trickery. I was later to get my wish in an amazing way, but meanwhile I found Bob still sitting with his back against a pillar, looking somewhat dazed by the afternoon's meeting.

"I was trying to draw in energy from the temple," he said, looking up at me, "But the more I tried, the weaker I seemed to become. My Yoga method didn't work and I don't know why."

I escorted him back to the room we had rented and he lay down on his mattress on the stone floor.

"I think I must sleep for a while," he said, wearily.

That afternoon I became acquainted with one *bhajan* singer in the temple, a young Bengali named Deb Kumar Ghosh. He told me that he was very close to Baba, so I asked about their relationship and whether Deb had any interesting stories to tell.

The young man opened up quite freely:

"Baba has given me everything. At one point I felt like I was almost a part of him, I loved him so much. Then I had news from Calcutta that my elderly father was ill. I asked Baba for leave to visit my family. He smiled broadly at me and said 'You will need money for your train fare.' Then he waved his hand in the air and suddenly materialised a hundred-rupee note and gave it to me. I could hardly believe my eyes, but there it was more than enough for my round trip fare with extra to buy food."

"Tell me more about your relationship with Baba," I asked.

"You will think me mad," Deb replied, "But one day Baba asked me to hug him. 'Squeeze me tightly,' he said, 'and feel the bliss of Heaven from where I come.' I put my arms around Baba and my face close to his, and I began to feel dizzy with happiness. I can't explain to you just how peaceful and how wonderful I felt. Baba asked me gently: 'What do you want from me? I can give you anything.' Many things went through my mind, but I ended up saying 'I just want to be with you, Baba.' Then he touched every part of my body and blessed me. Never in my whole life before have I felt so near to God. Baba is like a father and a mother to us all."

Deb was completely sincere in his explanation. I did not find it difficult to accept that God is male and female, negative and positive, and that within Baba there is a perfect balance of the two. So often I had heard Baba described as being like a mother. He has frequently been known to serve food to his devotees. I thought of Jesus washing the disciples' feet. There seemed to be many parallels.

By the morning of the fourth day I was becoming extremely anxious to have an interview with Baba. Bob and I had sat for many hours on the sand under the coconut trees waiting for Baba at least to look at us, but he passed us by. We spoke to a European man who worked in the temple. He was dressed in Indian costume. We asked him to help us obtain an interview. He was sympathetic but said, "I'm sorry I can do nothing. Only Baba can call you." And so it was.

We had decided to wait four days before returning to Bangalore and then flying back to Bombay. Bob wished to continue with his healing work there, and a Spiritualist group in Bombay had asked me to demonstrate clairvoyance before I left for England. Bob was becoming impatient sitting for hours in the ashram doing nothing. I understood his frustration. When Baba appeared on that last occasion he did not approach us. In desperation I got out of my place, took my cine camera, and darting round the back of a low wall I ran quickly along to the spot where Baba was giving *darshan*. From over the top of the wall I began filming him. Suddenly he looked up in my direction and I heard a strange click from my camera. I continued filming however until the indicator showed the footage was complete. When I opened my camera to change the reel, I noticed to my dismay that the film was stuck. None of those last valuable moments had been recorded. I was shocked and disappointed. I immediately knew that Baba had disapproved of my filming at that particular time, though strangely enough not earlier. I was puzzled by this and somewhat sad. Was Baba chiding me for my impatience? Perhaps I shall never know. I had never before had any trouble with that camera. It had always worked perfectly, but I do know that the timing of that fault was most peculiar. The strange clicking sound had happened at exactly the moment Baba looked at me.

After Baba disappeared into his private room to continue giving interviews, the resident European asked if I would care to do some work for the temple. I willingly agreed, as I was sorry if I had displeased Baba by my actions. I was merely human, and trying to make the most of my final afternoon at the ashram.

A large water pond surrounding a tall lotus column needed emptying. With many other people we formed a chain gang and passed buckets of water to the rhythmical chant of '*Sai Ram.*' The green water from the lotus pond refreshed every tree and bush in the sandy compound. We worked for a solid three hours in the hot sun, yet never once did I feel thirsty. My fellow workers were Americans, Japanese, Malaysians and Indians. It was a truly cosmopolitan situation, one I shall never forget.

That evening we took a taxi to Bangalore and Bob insisted on being driven to the airport where he bought two seats on a small Indian Airbus returning to Bombay. I pleaded with him to return by train as I could see how dark and overcast the sky had become. It was monsoon season and I had a bad feeling about the flight. My premonition proved to be only too accurate, for within a few minutes after take-off we were tossed about mercilessly in the air in what proved to be the worst turbulence I had ever experienced. I was leaning forward in my seat, crying out and gasping for breath each time the plane dropped. I was literally terrified. Bob seemed unaffected by the turbulence and he did his best to comfort me, but by the time we landed at Bombay, I was feeling extremely sick and heartily glad to see our friends the kind Mahadevia family who waited to greet us.

Fortunately my recovery was rapid and we were able to visit the healing sanctuary of a Miss Patel, whose father had once been Bob's guru. At her sanctuary many people were gathered for Bob to again demonstrate his wonderful powers of magnetic healing.

Later, I also conducted a séance for a Bombay Spiritualist group, struggling to bring through the difficult names; but with some degree of success.

I still believe that Sathya Sai Baba contributed much to the field of education in his country, and that most of the devotees were dedicated and sincere people. However, I cannot help but feel that being in human form also makes a 'god man' subject to human desires and human failings. There was the continued enigma of Baba's sexuality. There have been many allegations that Baba had asked young European men to drop their pants during private interviews The young men (some of whom were married) claimed that their genitals were fondled and that Baba attempted to masturbate them under the guise of balancing their kundalini. It is claimed that one young man was so disturbed by 'God' doing this to him that he later committed suicide. Other allegations of Baba having favourite small boys from the college service him in his bedroom, were disturbing to say the least. Whatever Baba's sexual orientation may have been, it was certainly very inappropriate and illegal to involve young children. If these allegations were true, and not merely a part of some smear campaign, then I am completely bewildered by this information. It is not for me to judge but I do have serious nagging doubts about the true nature of this 'god man.' Several former devotees have also claimed that Baba had a large supply of rings and watches in his private room and that many of the so-called materialisations were achieved by sleight-of-hand. If such claims are true, then Baba can be no more than a talented magician or a man with some high degree of physical mediumship. Initially I was impressed by his appearance and by what happened at Whitefields, but now I find myself puzzled. I was certainly left with a feeling of disappointment that my precious film had been ruined on that final afternoon at Puttaparthi. How it happened, only Heaven or Baba knows.

Here I am lecturing on English teaching methods at the B.M. Institute of Mental Health in Ashram Road, Ahmedabad. In the background is the Principal of Gujarat University. Years later did an acrylic painting based upon this photograph while studying at Los Angeles City College.

32.

Back in England I continued my work for the Spiritualist Movement. I became one of the Trustees of the Huntingdon Spiritualist Church and joined the band of healers. Soon Bob announced that we would be adding some new rooms to the back of the church as he was negotiating bringing a young couple from Australia who had the ability to perform bare-hand psychic surgery.

Previously, Bob and his wife Ann had travelled to the Philippines with friends Tom and Joan Williams. There at the Bay View Hotel in Manila and at various places in Pangasinan, they had witnessed the most incredible things. Bob had made a super 8mm film recording some of these bare-hand healings by the different psychic surgeons. Tom Williams had lectured at the church and shown his own movies of these 'impossible' happenings. I was deeply impressed by what I had seen. The body was apparently opened up without the aid of any scalpel. Large tumours and pieces of dark, blood-like tissue were effortlessly removed from the patients being treated. Now Bob informed us about the husband-and-wife team who were to arrive from Sydney, Australia, to demonstrate their healing powers in a private capacity and also as guests of the Spiritualists' National Union.

In November 1977, London's *Psychic News* first ran an article about David and Helen Elizalde. Geoff and Mollie Wilde, an Australian couple who had received healing, had been so impressed by the results that they set out to publicise the work of David and Helen. Geoff Wilde, aged 72, took photographs of the psychic surgery to the Editor of *Psychic News* and outlined a plan to bring the couple to England the following spring so that their work could be observed by experts. Bob Copley contacted the healers direct and also offered to finance their visit and provide them with hospitality at his beautiful home in Hemingford Grey.

The first time this lovely couple walked down the aisle of the Huntingdon Spiritualist Church and were introduced to the congregation by Bob I knew I was about to experience something quite unique. David had typical Philippino features, and was a strong, athletic young man in his thirties. He had been a karate champion and had also undergone two years' training as a policeman. Helen, his wife, had long black hair in a bouffant style and the beautiful olive skin of a Greek-Cypriot. I learned later she had been born in London and her father had owned the Apollo nightclub. As a small girl she had been sent to a Catholic boarding school in the country and had badly missed parental affection. She spoke with a British accent and had a gentle personality.

David was a cousin to the famous Tony Agpaoa, a Philippino who had made headlines by his psychic surgery on the rich and famous. Unfortunately Tony Agpaoa had garnered unfavourable publicity by his flamboyant lifestyle and egotistical behaviour. David sought to distance himself from his cousin's image by using his mother's maiden name of Elizalde instead of the family name of Agpaoa.

Helen, I learned, had been previously married to an Australian doctor. She had worked in a beauty parlour where she had given facial massages to wealthy clients. Those who suffered from skin diseases found that their conditions cleared up after Helen had worked on them. Through this occupation she began to discover her healing gifts. She lived a privileged life but was not totally happy. One day while under anaesthetic at the dentist's, she had an out-of-the-body experience in which she met a spiritual guide who told her to go and work among the poor in the Philippines. This visitation was so overpowering that she told her husband of the experience and asked him to accompany her. He was naturally reluctant to leave his successful practice, so Helen Morgante later flew to Manila by herself. There, at the Bay View Hotel she first met David who was working as a security officer and part-time healer. They teamed up and Helen herself developed the ability to separate the flesh by pointing her finger at the body of a patient. She claimed that a spirit voice guided her in the correct location and in the diagnosis of the particular ailment.

David and Helen opened up several healing clinics that eventually closed through lack of funds. The couple experienced extreme poverty and often had little food to eat. Ultimately Helen was divorced and free to marry David. A wealthy Italian benefactor whose brain tumour had been removed by the couple arranged for them to leave the Philippines and settle once more in Australia. There, Helen gave birth to twins. During their visit to England the young couple left their babies in the care of family members in the Philippines. It was necessary for them to earn money to support not only themselves but also various elderly members of David's family who were unable to work. Bob Copley with typical generosity sent money to Manila to assist the young couple and those who were dependent upon them.

The day arrived for David and Helen to begin their work at the Huntingdon Spiritualist Church. Gleefully, Bob Copley told me that he had already had a demonstration the previous evening when they had invited a local doctor in to see the couple at work.

The doctor had become very nervous when he saw blood and other matter removed from the body of an elderly man who had agreed to be the guinea pig. "They definitely go into the body," the astonished doctor said. Shortly after this demonstration he left Bob's home in quite a hurry obviously disturbed by what he had witnessed.

I stood waiting outside the church healing rooms with my Polaroid camera and also a 35mm camera, hoping and praying that I would be allowed to photograph the procedures. I need not have worried because Helen looked straight at me and said "You can come in and photograph us at work, as long as the patients don't object."

What an opportunity to witness first hand things I had only heard about or read of in books! The new healing rooms had just been completed with raised platform beds for the benefit of the patients. A qualified nurse, Mrs. Norma Flood was in attendance. Hot water was available for washing hands. David and Helen brought in bottles of olive oil, which they rubbed upon their fingers before touching the bare flesh of the patient. I noticed that Helen did not remove her wristwatch or ring.

"The energy we use prevents any infection," she explained confidently.

A lady wearing only panties and a bra lay on the bed. Joan Williams stood at the head of the bed and held the nervous lady's hands. A Bible lay on a nearby table within view of the patient. With lightly oiled fingers the couple began gently touching the abdominal area where the lady had experienced pain. While Helen's fingertips magnetised the flesh, I suddenly observed David's hand sink into the area below the navel. The woman flinched. David's hand began moving about inside the body, and the next moment he pulled out what appeared to be a large lump of gristle covered with blood. This he flopped into a bowl. I quickly photographed the procedure. There was a sudden unpleasant smell that caused us all to screw up our noses. For a moment I felt a little faint. There was no doubt that the bad smelling substance had been removed from the lady. Whether it was a piece of undigested meat trapped in the bowel or something else, I have no way of knowing. The couple had brought nothing into the church with them and I had watched very closely as the 'operation' took place.

For the next few days I was present at several hundred of these 'operations', recording the extraordinary events with my two cameras. Although I retained some of the photographs taken, most of the people wanted to take a Polaroid picture away with them as documentation of what had happened. They merely paid a small donation towards the cost of the film and that was it! My pictures went with the patients. Later, I wished I had had copies made of each photo before allowing it out of my possession, but the people were so insistent at the time I could hardly deny them their immediate proof of what had happened. I am sure that many of my Polaroid pictures are still treasured by family members to this day.

What kind of 'operations' did the young couple perform? Many were on the abdominal area. One lady who had been trying to get pregnant for some years received treatment from Helen who apparently unblocked the Fallopian tubes so that pregnancy could occur. I was not able to follow up on this, so do not know whether the lady eventually got her wish. Several times I saw blood materialise on the abdomen of the patient being treated. One moment the skin was clean, the next moment blood was clearly visible and had to be swabbed away either by the healer or the attendant nurse, Mrs. Flood.

A lady brought her mentally challenged young son for treatment from Helen. I stood watching everything. The boy sat in a chair and Helen, with upturned palm, was about to touch the back of his neck to give some magnetic healing. Suddenly I noticed that a lump of liver-like substance had appeared on her outstretched palm where there had been nothing just a second earlier. Helen reacted with some surprise, shrugged slightly and dropped the substance into one of the bowls. Samples of these substances were later tested and found to be genuine human tissue.

Dr. Alfred Stelter in his book *'Psi-Healing'* believed that it may be possible for a bioplasmic energy which takes the shape of human blood and tissue to be withdrawn from the body; and it is this, he theorised, that contains the seeds of the illness. Analysis has shown that *some* of the substances removed were not exactly of the human form. This led to allegations of fraud and the absurd suggestion by the magician James Randi that the healers concealed animal blood and organs in condoms concealed up their sleeves or in their palms. He also suggested that they used false thumbs to add to the illusion! What idiotic suggestions! Randi was never present at one of these operations and is not qualified to make any statement about them. *I* was there, and I wish to state quite emphatically that David and Helen Elizalde did not resort to *any* kind of trickery while demonstrating their unique healing gifts.

One lady, Mrs. Kathy Runham of Cambridge, had a large lump dissolved instantly from her breast by Helen. That is something a fraud just cannot do! I later spoke to the surgeon at Addenbrookes Hospital who had previously done a partial mastectomy on

278

that lady. He looked at my photographs with wonderment and commented:

"I'm sorry I cannot be drawn into this controversy. Until a patient has actually died and the autopsy reveals no trace of cancer we cannot say that a cure has been effected."

Obviously the orthodox medical view is that such things do not exist!

Several of the more hair-raising operations I witnessed were those performed on people's eyes. An elderly man lay on the platform bed and I watched, somewhat squeamishly, as David's index finger went under the man's eyelid and deftly removed the eyeball. As I leaned forward to take a closer look, I could see the optic nerve attached to the back of the protruding eye. Then David appeared to peel away a thin skin from the surface of the eyeball and just as quickly popped the organ back into its socket! David showed me the cataract he had just removed, sticking to the end of his finger. Afterwards the man said he could see more clearly, but he had felt some slight pain during the operation. I could well believe him. It looked like a most uncomfortable procedure!

A number of people lay belly down with a small towel covering their bare buttocks. I watched astonished as David, with oiled fingers, inserted his hand deep into the rectum and removed some large haemorrhoids, some of which looked like small bunches of grapes. Several people reported pain during the procedure; others said they felt nothing but a slight pressure. For reasons of modesty I was not permitted to photograph these particular operations. But 'seeing is believing' and I have no doubt that the people were healed of their painful haemorrhoids.

My mother, who was suffering from high blood pressure and some abdominal pain, lay on the raised bed in the healing room. She wore only her bra and panties and had a towel wrapped around the lower part of her body. I stood there with my Polaroid camera ready to record whatever the healers might do. Helen chose to do the procedure, as David was busy with another patient in the next room. I watched Helen put oil on her fingers and begin kneading the area below my mother's navel. The next moment Helen's hand was seen to slide deeply into the body and I saw my mother flinch as this happened. While keeping the body open with her left hand, Helen inserted the fingers of her right hand into the same area and withdrew some large clots of blood and bad-smelling matter. I took five Polaroid pictures of my mother's surgery. In one picture there is a curious streak of blue light that seems to originate from the top left hand corner and then descends diagonally to Helen's left sleeve. I am wondering whether my photo captured some of the bioelectrical energy involved in this amazing process. My mother said afterwards that she had felt Helen's hand deep inside her and that it was most uncomfortable. When the surgery had finished, there was a white line visible at the spot where Helen had entered the body. It took about twenty-four hours for this line to fade. My mother said that her abdominal pain had completely gone, although she felt a little sore for a day or two. Later that week, she made a routine visit to her own doctor. He was quite surprised to find that her blood pressure was normal and she seemed to be in good physical shape. She told me she had said nothing about her strange experience to the doctor! He wouldn't have believed her!

Was every case of psychic surgery successful? Apparently it was not. As Helen wisely said: "Many of these conditions have taken some time to develop so may need a series of magnetic healing treatments after the impurities have been withdrawn. We can only initiate the process of healing. People do not always follow a healthy life style or want to make major adjustments to their diet, so in that way we have limitations in what we can achieve for them. Some illnesses are also of a karmic nature and we cannot interfere with that soul's learning experience."

David and Helen gave treatment to a blind family who attended the church regularly. I was not present during those sessions, but the healers were unable to restore the sight of these hopeful patients. A man suffering from multiple sclerosis showed no apparent change after the treatment. He died a few years later. Another lady whose body was deformed through osteoarthritis was also unable to get relief from the condition. The greatest success seemed to be where soft, fatty tissue was involved. The couple was great at dissolving goitres, tumours and suchlike appendages. David, who merely pointed his finger at me, instantly dissolved a small, painful lump I had beneath my skin. That was impressive, I can assure you! It was my personal proof of the reality of their gift.

After a week of healing at Huntingdon, David and Helen left for the Arthur Findlay College at Stansted Hall just outside the village of Stansted Mountfitchet in Essex. There, at this wonderful mansion built by Spiritualist author Arthur Findlay, they continued to demonstrate psychic surgery while various members of the media were allowed in at different times to witness the procedures.

Encounters with the media were mostly unfortunate! *Psychic News* bravely defended the healers, rightly questioning why in the face of such physical proof of extraordinary healings, the media was so hostile. British Broadcasting Corporation Producer Christopher Mann said: "The operations are very convincing. The evidence of my eyes is consistent with them being genuine or a very clever conjuring trick. One can hypothesise that they heal psychosomatically and do a conjuring trick as a visible symbol."

What nonsense!

In 1979 David and Helen returned to England. Huntingdon Spiritualist Church was again blessed by their wonderful services. No patient was charged a single penny and Bob Copley provided hospitality and aid to the couple. Once again I photographed many of the procedures. I became very friendly with David and Helen, did their birth charts for them and spent many hours questioning them about their wonderful talents. Then it was once again time for them to leave for Stansted Hall.

The BBC had been negotiating with the Arthur Findlay College to allow cameramen in to film the psychic surgeries. After promising the college that they would not resort to calling in magicians or people of such calibre, the BBC team from 'Nationwide' was allowed to record some of the events. Helen was most encouraged when two of the cameramen told her: "This has to be genuine. We believe it!"

Then came the bombshell when the programme was shown on British television during prime time. The first ten minutes seemed very supportive of what the healers were doing. People were interviewed making positive remarks about their experiences. But the tone of the programme soon changed. American magician James Randi gave a not-very-convincing demonstration of how he believed the healers achieved their results through concealing blood in rubber balloons. One man, who had apparently been told that his kidney stones had been dissolved, had an X-ray after the procedure that showed the stones were still there. He was angry and out to expose what he felt was a trick performed upon him. I am certain that there was no deliberate intent to cheat this man, but in a cruel finale to the programme David and Helen were branded "confidence tricksters, unscrupulous frauds and liars exploiting the chronically sick."

Both David and Helen had tremendous faith in their spirit guides. When I visited them at Stansted Hall after the mischievous programme had been shown, Helen was crying. "We only tried to help people," she said, "We are not frauds, as you know, Brian."

I reassured the couple that I had total confidence in their authenticity. One of the problems with this type of healing is that there cannot be any hard and fast guarantees of cure. Helen said to me: "Some people are just negative and do not respond at all, no matter what we do."

In spite of sharp criticism by a few people and most of the media, I stand by the healers to this day. They did their best and sometimes they failed. Who can blame them for trying? The motive was good. They helped many people who readily testified to getting relief from their pain and discomfort, and the couple certainly did *not* earn "thousands of pounds" as several newspapers had suggested. I happen to know as an insider that their take-home pay was rather meagre, considering that they paid expenses for Geoff and Molly Wilde, the elderly Australian couple who accompanied them and who originally promoted their work in the United Kingdom. Geoff and Molly also assisted David and Helen in some of the operations. Stansted Hall charged only ten pounds for each patient, and those patients were allowed up to three treatments from the healers. London's *Psychic News* printed many testimonials from people who had been miraculously healed of severe conditions. There were also many explicit photographs in that truthful newspaper. I personally defended the healers on the front page as I was so outraged by the rude and vicious treatment they had received from the media. The BBC team of *Nationwide* was mistaken in its judgement, and hopefully those responsible for such cruelty to a wonderful couple will live to regret it! The sad consequences were that the Director of Public Prosecutions warned David and Helen that they could be arrested if they ever returned to England.

Nurse Norma Flood, David, myself and Helen Elizalde.

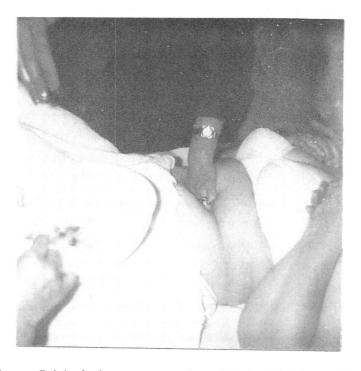

Above: Original photo was a coloured Polaroid. My mother felt the hand of Helen Elizalde deep inside her abdominal area where she had had a previous hysterectomy some years earlier. She had been experiencing pain and was concerned about a possible return of the cancer that had been removed.

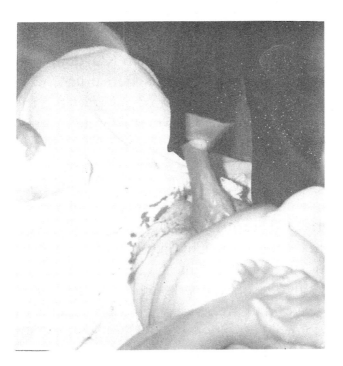

Above: In this Polaroid picture a streak of light can be seen descending from the top left hand corner towards Helen's hand as she begins to withdraw a blood-like substance from my mother's abdomen. After this rather uncomfortable procedure my mother had no further pain and her blood pressure was back to normal. She survived for a number of years until the cancer returned in 1984 when she finally passed into spirit.

33.

In August 1980 I left the United Kingdom to enter California State College in San Bernardino, where I completed my degree. I married an American friend. She was a good lady, but we rapidly discovered we had little in common, and for various reasons the marriage failed. As she is a rather private person I must respect her wishes and will say nothing further.

Meanwhile I had been corresponding with friends from India. I learned that the Jani family who had been my opposite neighbours in Ahmedabad were now mostly settled in Chicago and Washington DC. The youngest son Ramesh, who had helped me a great deal during my residency in India, told me that he was finally coming to the United States, under sponsorship from a family member. I was delighted to hear this, as Ramesh had been very supportive of my work as a medium and had sometimes sat with me in the Ahmedabad circle. His own mother, remember, was liable to fall into trances and to give messages to the family, so he was quite familiar with the subject. For a time Ramesh resided with his older brother in Chicago. It was wintertime and there was thick snow. He tramped the streets day after day looking for suitable work, but could not find it. Disillusioned, he wrote to me and I suggested that he join me in California. He arrived at Ontario airport on St. Patrick's Day and we celebrated after his arrival.

A tall, kindly man named Everett Harding, who had lost his only son tragically, offered us accommodation in the rear part of his home at Manhattan Beach. I had been successful in contacting Everett's beloved son and he was deeply grateful for the comfort my messages had provided. Everett's wife Margaret turned out to be a talented astrologer and we had many lively conversations on the subject. Later, I invited these kind people to England as my guests, and after the sad death of my mother from cancer in September 1984, my father was able to take a vacation in California and stay at the apartment in Manhattan Beach.

Meanwhile, Ramesh found employment almost immediately and I worked for a time in the office of a Jewish Mortuary and later in a doctor's office. Both jobs were interesting and I learned a great deal about the American way of doing things!

I began to receive requests for private sittings. Ultimately I took the plunge and decided to work only as a medium. There seemed to be an enormous hunger for the information and evidence I was able to provide. Word got around quickly and I was busy on a daily basis. I also did a great deal of travelling in the Greater Los Angeles area, visiting groups in their homes. But it was at the Hardings' Manhattan Beach house that I first met two of my long-term friends, Jay North, who played Dennis the Menace on television, and James Van Praagh, a short, jolly young man with an infectious laugh. James, in his best-selling book *'Talking to Heaven'* relates how he first came for an appointment with his boss Carol Shoemaker from the William Morris Agency, and how he was rather suspicious of the whole thing. It is ironic that years later James turned out to be one of America's most famous mediums! I was the first one to tell him of his potential talent and to encourage him in his psychic development. James brought various members of his family from New York to sit with me. In his third book '*Healing Grief*' he relates how I brought through evidence to his father Alan, and surprised everybody with the unexpected. James has always graciously acknowledged that meeting me changed his whole life!

Later, I was offered a duplex apartment in Irving Boulevard, just south of Paramount Pictures Film Studio, and there I was privileged to meet a number of movie stars and other television personalities who sought my aid. My duplex was situated next door to a larger house owned by Mr. Louis Federici, who at that time was the owner of a Los Angeles cinema. Louis provided hospitality each year to a famous English medium. The medium was none other than Leslie Flint. Leslie, who I have written about previously, was a great fan of the silent cinema and especially of the movies of Rudolph Valentino. Leslie had his own collection of those movies and also his own private cinema at his home in London. He had been highly thrilled when the voice of Valentino had manifested in his séance room over the years and given extraordinary information. Valentino once told Leslie that the two of them had been brothers in a previous incarnation in Italy and that was why Leslie felt drawn to the movie star. Leslie and I were able to get together again after many years. He was a kind, fatherly sort of man and highly supportive of the work I was doing in Los Angeles. I was invited to sit again in several of the dark room séances that were always held at Louis' house. Leslie had officially retired from the Spiritualist scene in London and only gave the occasional séance for friends. I was therefore very privileged to be included in these intimate gatherings. I got to know a small group of Leslie's friends and was always highly entertained by Leslie's secretary, Bram Rogers, who was a marvellous raconteur! Bram had quite a theatrical manner about him. He admitted that his education had been limited and he had been trained as a tailor, but he had such an enthusiasm for the theatre and the people in it that he had managed to meet many celebrities. He had worked for Leslie for many years after Leslie's wife Edith had died. Bram arranged the groups in London, threw the parties and generally was a lively master of ceremonies. A gregarious Aquarius, Bram surely had a Leo ascendant! He shone when he was centre stage and he certainly knew how to amuse an audience. Sometimes he got a little upset if anyone dared to interrupt his performance. Leslie by contrast was fairly quiet and would often self-consciously request that Bram not tell a certain story because it might be embarrassing! Once Bram related how a black man broke into their London house one night. Forcing them both into a bathroom, the burglar tied their hands behind their backs and made them lie on the floor while he searched for money. Leslie became very distressed and was groaning loudly while lying on his stomach. Highly concerned, Bram trussed up like a turkey kept talking to Leslie:

"Leslie are you all right? Are you feeling ill?" And then with some desperation said to the burglar: "You must untie him! Can't you see he's ill? Have you no heart?" The burglar apparently was somewhat touched. Kneeling down beside Leslie he also began saying: "Are you all right, Leslie? Are you feeling ill?" When Leslie made no reply the burglar locked the two of them in the bathroom and fled with a few valuables. Bram said they were left in that uncomfortable position all night until a shocked friend released them in the morning. Bram said that his own version of a funny song kept going through his mind:

"Oh dear, what can the matter be?
Leslie and Bram were locked in the lavatory,
They were there from Sunday to Saturday.
Nobody knew they were there!"

Leave it to Bram to turn a potentially tragic situation into one of high comedy!

Above: Medium Leslie Flint and close friend Bram Rogers.

Above: Ramesh at Valentino's tomb. They both share the same birthday by coincidence.

34.

I was fortunate enough to attend a number of Leslie's séances at Irving Boulevard. Apart from having some amusing conversations with the cockney guide Mickey, I also spoke to the spirit voice of the Nobel prize-winning physicist, Sir Oliver Lodge, who had died in 1940. He said that he had known of me for some years in his world. As a young man I had often visited The College of Psychic Science in London, and I suspect that Sir Oliver's spirit may have seen me there at that time. When I asked Sir Oliver whether he still saw his son Raymond, who had been killed in the First World War, I sensed irritation from the great man. Perhaps he thought I was testing him out by referring to Raymond, but he became very annoyed:

"Of course I've seen Raymond! What on earth are you on about?"

I was intending to ask whether young men who died in battle would need to reincarnate sooner, but the great man's impatience prevented me from following through with that question. Quickly I tried to smooth him over by stating that I had a copy of his book.

"I dare say you have!" he replied rather abruptly.

He had written a book titled *'Raymond, or Life and Death'* in which he testified to receiving evidence of his son's survival through various mediums, including Mrs. Gladys Osborne Leonard, one of the star mediums of her day. The book became a classic of psychic literature. I thought the great man still seemed very human, even from the other side!

Another communicator was the celebrated English actress Dame Ellen Terry. She had died in 1928, ten years before my birth, but her beautiful voice was clearly heard speaking in the air above Leslie's head. She sounded so kind and sweet. She told me that she was very interested in my work and that I should continue to tell people in my world that "death is the biggest illusion of the lot!" She went on to give us a rendition of Portia's speech from Act IV, scene one of *The Merchant of Venice*:

'The quality of mercy is not strained,
It droppeth as the gentle rain from heaven
Upon the place beneath: it is twice blest;
It blesseth him that gives and him that takes:
'Tis mightiest in the mightiest: it becomes
The throned monarch better than his crown..."

She still remembered her lines perfectly in spite of having been 'dead' for so many years.

At one séance a well-educated female voice manifested. She said her name was Florence Hurst and that she was a member of my family and she had lived in London with her husband John. They had been married in 1827 and her maiden name had been Fletcher. She told me that she had once been an actress, and John's family had been somewhat prejudiced against her because of her connection with the theatre. She and John "got along very well." She told me she had died sometime in the eighteen eighties in Eastbourne on the south coast of

England and she was very interested in me because I was interested in Spiritualism. She commented that I was a very extraordinary young man: nowadays, not so young! One day perhaps I will have time to research some of Florence's information. It was all quite precise.

Perhaps the most convincing message was one received from my Uncle Henry. He had been married to my mother's older sister Elsie. They lived in a small house in Montagu Road, Huntingdon. Henry had died after complications from diabetes and an amputation of his leg. He spoke to me in his exact earthly voice and gave me a very nice message from my dead mother. I thought that was particularly gracious of him as he had always made fun of my mother's belief in Spiritualism. While on her way to a Sunday service at the local Spiritualist Church my mother would often call at Elsie's house for a cup of tea. Henry would always be stretched full length on the only sofa and would not offer to move. Sometimes he would be sarcastic:

"Ha! Going to talk to the spirits are you? Give them a glass of whiskey from me!"

My mother would usually tell him to "shut up!"

To his credit he did convey a beautiful message through Leslie's wonderful mediumship. I could go on with many examples. I can only assure my reader that everything I have written is true. I have a good memory and tape-recorded sessions of these séances to back up all my claims.

There is no doubt whatsoever that the spirit world exists, that each one of us will one day pass into it and be subject to instant rejuvenation and freedom from disease. However, before you decide to end your earthly life this instant, take note that there is compensation for all good done here and retribution for evil.

There are many different levels on the other side, and to avoid ending up in the darker spheres in some kind of collective nightmare, it is best that we develop our ability to be of service to others and that we love all people regardless of race, colour or creed. That is the best advice I can give you! Suicide may be excused through mental illness and chemical imbalance, and help is usually given by spirits accustomed to work with such conditions. Some suicides are stunned to find that they haven't ended their existence and they are then called upon to face up to the issues that drove them to such a desperate measure. If they are open to persuasion, they can usually be assisted out of the earthbound condition their mental state may have imposed upon them. In some cases, unfortunately, stupid pride and a fixed attitude may take time to overcome! Sometimes suicides will refuse to communicate at a séance because they feel so thoroughly ashamed of all the pain they have caused their loved ones. It may take much patience and persistence to get any kind of message from them at all. I advise the grieving loved ones on earth to light candles and say prayers and send love to those distressed souls. All that mental and spiritual energy does reach them and eventually helps to release them from their torment. No one is condemned forever. Pain does ultimately end. All souls in darkness will one day come into the light, and what joy there will be awaiting them. But first there must be remorse for wrongdoing and a desire to rectify the negative way of thinking.

This photo was taken by Ramesh in 1987 at the Mausoleum in the Hollywood Forever Cemetery. In the background is the tomb of movie star Rudolph Valentino. Leslie would often visit this peaceful place as it was within walking distance of Mr. Louis Federici's home in Irving Boulevard where Leslie was, by all of us, a much-welcomed regular guest.

35.

In October 1992 I bought my own home in Yarmouth Avenue, Reseda where I began to hold group meetings on the first Saturday of the month. The house had a large room extending from front to back and this proved useful in seating the numerous people who attended each group. Soon the media started taking an interest.

Earlier I had appeared on channel 4's programme *'The Other Side'*, hosted by Dr. Will Miller. I had been extremely nervous to be on national television for the first time, but to their credit the editors of the show made me look good. James Van Praagh also appeared on the show and was their 'star medium.' Later, *'Hard Copy'* and *'Extra'* approached me and teams from both shows were admitted to the monthly group at different times for recording of the events. *'Hard Copy'* was respectful and showed a positive approach to the subject, whereas *'Extra'* brought in the debunker, Michael Shermer, to call me a fraud and a scam. To their credit, however, *'Extra'* did allow me the last word. I said "If I am attacked (and I knew I would be) there's a whole army of people out there who will defend me because *they* know that I'm genuine."

I said that because I knew instinctively from the attitude of the producer of that segment that she was a total sceptic and was out to 'get me.' She almost fell asleep in my rocking chair during taping of the group meeting. The cameramen, however, were great guys and both said that they believed in me because of what they had witnessed that evening.

Jane Berwick, a delightful talk show hostess who had her own programme on Pasadena cable named '*Answers,*' also interviewed me, together with some of my clients who testified to the specific proof I had provided them of communication with the spirit world. We did four half-hour segments, portions of which I am told were extremely moving. Mrs. Inger Rothenborg, a Danish lady whose innocent young mountaineer son had been murdered, testified to how I had given specific names and details that could only have come from her dead son. For some time she had tried desperately to get justice for the murder of Ken by hiring private investigators. Ken had been tricked into entering a private home in the Yosemite area, ostensibly to check out the electrical supply. There he had been set upon, beaten, and sadistically tortured by a couple of perverts who had then stripped him, raped him and thrown his mutilated body from the top of a waterfall in Yosemite National Park. Inger told me that the very first time she saw me I actually spelled out the name of the killer. She had discovered that these evil men had been police drug informants, and as such, she claimed, were under police protection. She, herself, got into trouble for even trying to investigate them! What horrible pain Inger had been through! My heart went out to her immediately. She was a good friend of Doris Tate, mother of the murdered movie star Sharon Tate, and it was at Doris's home in

Rancho Palos Verdes that I had first made contact with the murdered Ken.

Through my friendship with Doris Tate I became involved with work for *The Parents of Murdered Children* and *The Compassionate Friends,* two bereavement support organisations. Doris was a warm and extremely kind lady who had received a number of awards from the State of California for her humanitarian services. These hung on the wall of her home in Monero Drive. In her comfortable sitting room I held a number of séances for parents of murdered children and Doris had great faith in my ability. Later, Doris was kind enough to invite me to a couple of the Star Mothers' dinners in Beverly Hills. There I photographed her in conversation with her friend actor Jack Palance. On stage, Debbie Reynolds was highly entertaining in her impersonation of Zsa Zsa Gabor slapping the cop in Beverly Hills, an event that had received much newspaper coverage. Debbie's performance brought the house down! I laughed so much I had tears running down my face! A year later, when I accompanied Doris to the same event, I remember having to steady that dear lady as she walked down the steps at the hotel. Sadly, the sinister brain cancer, which later killed her, was beginning to affect her coordination and her memory. Regrettably, I was unable to attend Doris's funeral as I was only informed of it the day before, and I had clients coming from a distance for a sitting and could not disappoint them. I am sure that Doris would have understood. We all miss this wonderful lady who did such sterling work for people who were in terrible pain. May God bless her always!

I also gave sittings to Doris's two daughters, Debra and Patty. Debra was a sceptic and Patty was not. I was told that the two sisters had quite a discussion after the first sitting with me. Later, Patty had a second private session and was very satisfied with the results. Sometime later Patty also passed to the higher life from cancer where I am sure she was reunited with her mother and sister Sharon. I was most thrilled and excited when Patty made contact through me with another family member at a subsequent sitting.

Other shows in which I have taken part are *'Beyond Death'*, a highly-rated two-hour documentary for television by Actuality Productions in association with Margaret Wendt, and The Learning Channel's *'Best Kept Secrets of the Paranormal'* first shown in the US in February 2001. Both these productions were extremely fair and balanced in their presentation of the subject matter. The public enjoyed them immensely and I received over a hundred telephone calls from interested people seeking further information.

Doris (Gwen) Tate with a young friend at the Star Mothers' Dinner in Beverly Hills, California and with actor friend Jack Palance.

36.

My Autobiography would be incomplete without a description of one of the most exciting events that could possibly happen to anyone working in this field. I am speaking here of extraordinary physical encounters with the spirit world in my own home.

It all began in March 1996 after I had booked a flight to England. My elderly father, Ken, had been in a convalescent home there for several years suffering from the effects of Parkinson's disease. My dear mother had passed much earlier in September 1984 of cancer. In the past I had regularly telephoned Dad at weekends. Now his condition was too severe and he was unable to hold a conversation for any length of time without becoming confused and forgetful. I missed our conversations. Dad had been a smart and intelligent man, a college teacher of shorthand and typewriting who had cared deeply for his children and always tried to instil a good sense of values in us.

I had just bought my plane ticket when I received a very interesting letter from a man named Robin Foy, who was a well-known lecturer on psychic research. Robin had been investigating physical mediumship for many years and he was seeking contacts in the United States. Immediately I phoned him, telling him of my impending trip. I was invited to sit with his group of mediums in a cellar known as 'the Scole hole' underneath a farmhouse in the village of Scole in Norfolk. This was an opportunity I could not miss!

After arrival at my brother Peter's home in St. Ives, Cambridgeshire, he agreed to drive me to Scole for the séance in the cellar. He was somewhat nervous, as he had never experienced that kind of phenomena, but when he met the four mediums at Street Farmhouse I could see him visibly relax.

The two trance mediums were Alan and Diana Bennett, a most friendly fair-haired couple in their early fifties. By profession Alan was a carpenter with a strong interest in electronics and Diana had once run a dog-grooming business between bringing up a family and helping her husband to build their own beautiful home. Robin was an ex-pilot who had worked as a sales representative for a Scandinavian paper company. At one time he and his wife Sandra had also owned a fish and chip shop. Both were strong physical mediums, and I eagerly anticipated the séance.

Eventually we descended a worn flight of stone steps into the brick cellar and sat on wooden chairs around a large circular table. It was somewhat chilly and Sandra had previously plugged in an electric fire to warm the atmosphere. Sandra sat to my left and Robin sat to the right of my brother. Robin operated a small tape recorder, which played relaxing music in the background. Alan and Diana were seated more or less opposite us, between Robin and Sandra. On the table we noticed various objects. There was a glass dome raised on a stand resting upon the table, and a bowl that had some luminous table tennis balls in it. Robin explained that energy could apparently be stored in the glass dome between sittings. I found this all very intriguing! Robin also mentioned that the luminous balls could be moved about if the spirits desired.

The lights were extinguished and the sitting began. Soon Alan and Diana were taken into trance and various personalities began communicating. Mrs. Bradshaw, a rather proper Victorian lady, made reference to Peter's health problems and also gave an excellent commentary on the different phenomena as it occurred. At one point she said: "There's a beautiful retriever dog here that would love to make your acquaintance. May we send her over to you?"

I immediately said "Yes," and heard my brother go "Uh oh!"

We heard the slight tap tap tap of a dog's claws on the brick floor and suddenly felt the dog materialise beside us, wagging its tail. The tail hit both our legs and was quite solid for a few moments. Peter said: "I wonder if it's our old dog Trixie?"

And as quickly as it had manifested, it had gone! I immediately knew it was not a dog hidden in a secret cupboard because you can't get rid of a friendly dog just like that!

Later the round table began vibrating strongly and from the luminous tabs placed upon it we could see that it was being raised about two feet from the floor. Soon the voice of a man named Reginald began speaking to us from high up near the ceiling. "I'll try and show myself to you!" he said.

Sure enough we could see a column of luminous mist begin to appear above the table top, and this formed the figure of a man, although we were not able to see his face. He talked to us for several minutes before the voice faded away. Peter was so much in awe of the whole experience he told me afterwards that he was unable to speak.

Throughout the séance, which lasted almost two hours, we were clearly able to see small round lights that flew about the room and hovered in front of our faces. The playful lights changed their position rapidly, at one point moving quickly under the table, up through its centre and into the glass dome. They buzzed around like some kind of insects, then just as quickly flew out and nudged the luminous table tennis balls in the small bowl. It was an astonishing display of spiritual energy!

An Indian man named Raji, came through Alan and began talking about the steam trains in India. I engaged him in conversation and informed him that I had ridden on those trains a number of times during my visits to India. Raji spoke English with a very authentic Indian accent and sounded quite different from Alan.

The highlight of the séance, however, was the gradual appearance of a tiny cluster of star-like lights that moved towards me in the dark. They reminded me somewhat of a luminous jellyfish as they approached. I was requested to put out my left hand, and as I did this, the tiny sparkling lights suddenly changed their shape. There, floating just in front of me was a greyish-looking hand that appeared to have a somewhat rough surface.

"It's Reginald. He wants to touch you," Sandra said.

Sure enough, the hand, which had a faint luminous quality, descended and began to stroke my palm. It was a very odd sensation, as the fingers were quite large and thick and felt callused, like those of a farmworker. They were also somewhat damp! I was certainly a little nervous, but resisted the urge to pull my hand away from the strange materialisation. Because of the greyish-blue colour I had a sudden amusing mental flash that the hand reminded me of 'the incredible hulk,' an American TV and cartoon character. Then the hand just seemed to melt away. Once again I saw the floating cluster of 'jellyfish' lights that gradually distanced themselves from me in the dark until they were no longer visible.

When the séance was over, the mediums took us up to a ground floor library where I noticed Robin had an excellent collection of classic psychic books. There Peter and I were treated to a slide show of strange pictures that had been received on unexposed film placed inside locked boxes in the cellar during various sittings. Professor Emeritus Arthur J. Ellison, a consultant engineer, Professor David Fontana and Mr. Montgomery Keen, all members of the Council of the British Society for Psychical Research, had been present during most of those sittings over a period of two years. Strict research protocol had been observed, making the possibility of fraud highly unlikely.

In my letter of thanks to Robin and his team I commented: "The slide display in your ground floor room, showing the unusual patterns and possible biological formations precipitated upon undeveloped film in the cellar, was mind-boggling. Some of the slides were extremely beautiful, would make wonderful posters, and whether they are 'thought forms' or 'energy displays,' the occasional 'pussycat's head' or human face or 'Rembrandt-like figure' provided enough visual excitement to challenge any display of modern art!" Samples of these astonishing psychic pictures may be seen on the Scole Experimental Group's website.

Above: The Scole Experimental Group. L to R: Robin Foy, Diana Bennett, Alan Bennett and Sandra Foy at Street Farmhouse, Scole, Norfolk, 1996.

Above: Robin Foy with glass dome that stored psychic energy.
Below: Diana and Alan Bennett, the two trance mediums.

After witnessing this amazing display of psychic energy I knew that I had to bring the mediums to California. I had been lecturing on physical mediumship for so many years that it was time to either 'put up' or 'shut up.' I chose to do the former, and Robin and his team arrived at my home in March 1997, ready to demonstrate before American audiences. We deliberately avoided involving the media and sent notices only to people who had some knowledge of or interest in this subject. Many of the sitters were drawn from my monthly lecture group. They were enthusiastic, open-minded and genuinely nice people. I did not wish the Scole Experimental Group to be subjected to ridicule, sarcasm or any kind of abuse from the press, as the mediums were my guests for the first time in California and I had to protect them.

My two-car garage was cleared of much of its junk, the ceiling insulated and linoleum and a red carpet placed on the concrete floor. I personally painted all the rafters and the walls, ridding the place of spiders and other undesirable creatures. The garage was the cleanest it had ever been! A perfect blackout had to be achieved and this was done with the help of plastic bags and insulating tape around the large garage door.

While I was preparing the environment for the sittings, I had a number of odd things happen. The sprinklers came on suddenly along the sidewalk at an unscheduled time. Checking the electronic control box there was no indication of any sprinkler activity whatsoever! This happened on three different occasions and all at different times of day. I began to wonder whether the spirits were letting me know in this playful manner that they were testing the energy before the mediums arrived! Battery-operated smoke alarms high on the walls of my home also went off at different times when there was no fire and absolutely no smoke!

During the three weeks that the mediums were my guests, over 160 people attended the different sittings in the blacked-out garage. I hung a wind chime from one of the rafters and Robin placed luminous tabs on the paddle of the wind chime. The group brought their own set of cowbells that were also hung from a rafter. In the centre of the room was a round wooden table I had purchased from a discount store. On the table top Robin had arranged four crystals to coincide with the four compass points. Two large quartz crystals were also placed in the centre. These magnetised rocks apparently aided the spirit people in their tasks. The table was also distinguishable in the dark by luminous tabs that Robin stuck to both top and underside. There were definitely no wires of any kind attached to the table because I carefully monitored the whole procedure. Each medium wore luminous armbands fastened with Velcro, so as to be clearly distinguished in the dark. All the mediums sat together at the south side of the garage, their backs to some large cupboards that could not be opened without moving the mediums. From left to right they were Sandra Foy, Alan Bennett, Diana Bennett and Robin Foy. At the first sitting on March 21st, 1997 and subsequently, Robin had a small folding table in front of him. On the table was a portable battery operated tape recorder. Robin also had there a collection of prerecorded tapes of different kinds of music from classical Strauss waltzes to modern jazz.

Each sitting opened with a few words from Manu, the guide and co-ordinator from the spirit realms. Speaking through Diana, he explained that there would need to be a blending of energies from the earth, from his own side and from the people present before the phenomena could occur. He spoke of 'love in action' and reassured the expectant audiences that he was a being of light. By creating a positive mental atmosphere all participants could then allow themselves to experience something quite unique.

Regular communicators, using Alan and Diana as spokespeople followed the more serious Manu. Mrs. Bradshaw, Edwin, Joseph and a very amusing Irishman named Patrick all manifested. Patrick particularly had the audience in stitches and helped them to relax and overcome any nervousness. After about thirty minutes of amusing and very clever patter by these different personalities, lights began to appear like shooting stars in the dark. The wind chime tinkled loudly for several minutes. The excitement of the audience reached a climax with a buzz of conversation and exclamations of "Wow!" and "Oh, my God!" at the amazing display of lights that flew rapidly about, made a figure eight and a smiley mouth, before darting under and around the chairs of the sitters. Next we heard an 'energy voice' from the air, high up near the garage roof. He said his name was Charles White and he was known on earth as 'Chalky'. Robin and some of the sitters conversed with him for less than a minute before the voice faded. Robin had explained earlier in his lecture to the group, prior to entering the garage that these voices do not use ectoplasm, but are produced in a completely different way. The voice was not very loud and sounded almost like someone speaking at the other end of a metallic pipe! As the American sitters verbalised their experiences to one another, Emily Bradshaw joked that she had learned some new phrases like 'double whammy' and 'surfing the net.' One lady complained that she was feeling extremely hot and Emily replied that the energy did vary from one location to another. Chalky White suddenly intervened from the air with the comment "Don't get the wind up!" to everyone's amusement.

Next there was an intense light display together with the wind chime tinkling loudly and the cowbells ringing from another location. One small light did a nosedive straight through the centre of the round table to the cry of "Oh my God!" from a man sitting near to it. The light even explored the area of Robin's tape recorder and he felt himself being touched. Next the light flew slowly around the garage and approached individual sitters, nudging them quickly and darting away. As the light skimmed through one lady's hair she asked, "Are you an E.T?" Another lady said the light moved down the whole length of her arm. "It feels wonderful!" she exclaimed enthusiastically.

A rather stifled energy voice again spoke in the air: "Can you hear me all right?"

A chorus of voices confirmed they could.

The spirit of a man named John spoke very briefly and there was a strange clicking noise in the air. Soon a light began exploring the boundaries of the garage, shooting above the rafters and going into the corners. Then the unpredictable light suddenly entered one of the crystals on the table, creating a distinct illumination for a few seconds. Joseph, speaking through Alan, asked the audience whether they were enjoying the experience. There was no doubt in anyone's mind that this was something quite unique! They were all glad they had come to Yarmouth Avenue. Joseph explained that because of the mediums' relatively short visit to California, the spirit team was endeavouring to show the audience a variety of phenomena that would not normally occur together in the cellar at Scole.

"There's going to be a change of focus now," he informed everyone.

Robin changed the taped music to some soft Mozart. Joseph then thanked Ramesh and I for allowing our home to be used by the spirit team. He also explained to the audience how they, the spirits, were endeavouring to create phenomena that could be repeated for the benefit of the investigating scientists in England. The table vibrated audibly. One lady commented that her hair was being stroked. Robin explained that all of these touches were loving, as the spirits did not wish to alarm anyone. The wind chime then played a simple tune, and some of the sitters applauded. There was an immediate loud response from a pair of spirit hands clapping vigorously from high up in the air in order to demonstrate their solidity at the time. Then, to the astonishment of everyone, the round, luminous-tabbed table was levitated up and between the rafters in the garage and slowly descended, while appearing to rotate. With a strange life of its own, the table then glided from one side of the circle to the other, gently nudging some sitters on their knees. People cried out in surprise as they felt the table touch them. Robin commented that this was the first full levitation they had experienced for two years. I made everyone laugh when I said that the table had come from 'Pic-N-Save' and had cost only twenty dollars! It was moved at every séance and the surprising thing was that the crystals on top were never disturbed.

Soon Emily Bradshaw announced that she and her team were ready to take some questions. James Van Praagh asked about the spiritual level from which the guides originated. Edwin, a philosopher speaking through Alan, informed James that the spirit controls had to be highly evolved in order to manipulate the energies of the universe, and so be of service to Mankind. There were a few deep comments about the nature of thought and energy, suggesting that the two be inextricably related. Edwin said that thoughts from the brain were human and earthly, relating to physical needs, whereas thoughts from the Mind originated from a higher level of consciousness. Ramesh, a Hindu, asked whether one had to return to earth even after reaching the highest spheres. Edwin replied: "No, I understand you are absorbed into the greater Mind."

Dr. Gary Schwartz of the University of Arizona, who is researching these things, believes in his book *'The Living Energy Universe'* that each one of us is helping 'God' to learn and evolve through our own thought, action and experience here on earth. I am inclined to agree with Dr. Schwartz. I think we are all part of a greater mind matrix, and that in spite of our apparent separateness we are all linked together at subtle levels, and what is done to each individual *does* matter. Many of the teachings of Hinduism and Buddhism make a great deal of sense and should, in my opinion, be incorporated into the Judaic and Christian philosophies.

Spiritualist author Arthur Findlay in his book *'The Curse of Ignorance'* reveals how the early Christians did accept reincarnation and many ideas of Eastern origin, but with the growth of a powerful priesthood the mediums and psychics began to be persecuted as witches and sorcerers by the jealous priests. The human ego and desire for power got in the way of true understanding. Jesus made a profound statement when he said, "By their *fruits* ye shall know them." There were obviously false prophets and true prophets as there are today, and all of this is in order to teach the fool to become wise and the investigator to be discerning. Meanwhile Joe Soap struggles on!

Our first séance in the garage ended with Emily urging all the sitters to be like candles in the dark, to be a blazing beacon of light for the good of the world. She said that in the future more people would be born with a greater understanding of these things and she was informed that a higher spirituality was coming to earth.

There was certainly nothing in the comment of the spirit intelligence that made me feel at all uneasy. The phenomena were wonderful, the messages were good and often very humorous, and the people were exhilarated during the extraordinary displays of light energy and levitation of the table.

Seven further sittings were equally successful with some sitters receiving a great variety of evidence through Alan and Diana's trance controls. Mrs. Bradshaw made reference to a young man who had been murdered and who was anxious to communicate with his mother who was not present at any of the sittings. The facts related to one of my clients whose son had been stabbed outside a Taco Bell restaurant in the city of Tarzana. I recognized the information immediately and was able to pass on the message to the grieving mother.

All in all, we made psychic history here on the West Coast of the United States and the spirits proved to all present that they did not need to be in the 'Scole hole' for results to occur.

The penultimate sitting was particularly outstanding and was attended by Mr. Monty Keen, the public relations officer of the British Society for Psychic Research. He sat in the dark with his pad and pencil taking notes in shorthand and the tiny light, by that time christened 'Tinkerbell' hovered

318

above him illuminating his pad as he wrote notes. The crystals were levitated and banged together, creating sparks and causing a small piece to split off and drop in a lady's lap. She kept it as a souvenir. The spirits pulled out all the stops to make that particular evening a tremendous success and the solid spirit hands and arms were felt at some time by most of the sitters. Particularly impressive was the entrance of the spirit lights into the bodies of various sitters. We learned afterwards that one man who was suffering from a major heart problem was instantly healed of it after the tiny light had penetrated his chest. Mrs. Tricia Loar of Glendale who had much pain in her knee and ankle reported a tickling sensation as the light entered both areas and she also was relieved of pain. She also testified that she had reached out in the dark at one point and felt a warm hand. Anxious to discover more she groped her way up a hairy arm to the shoulder area and found nothing there. It was a disembodied arm that had touched her.

Movie star Kathryn Grayson attended one of the sittings together with popular singer Tom Cooper. Kathryn reported being kissed on the lips by her dead sister. Many sitters also reported being touched.

The only useable entrance to the garage was via Ramesh's small bedroom. I sat with my back to the closed bedroom door during each sitting as I was operating a tape recorder of my own, using a sensitive floor microphone which picked up everything quite clearly. At different séances a furry cat with a long tail and also a friendly dog materialised and walked about the garage, rubbing against the legs of various sitters who responded with excitement and surprise. A small child named Carrie also materialised her tiny fingers and arms and walked around touching a number of people, including my friend Jay North (Dennis the Menace of TV fame). There was no way in which any physical animal or child could have had access to my garage, except through the door which I was blocking! We all had positive proof that the spirit world can interact with ours and that the 'dead' can have a wonderful sense of humour!

I am extremely proud of the Scole Experimental Group. They accepted the tremendous challenge to demonstrate in another country at the home of someone they had only met once. They showed a supreme act of faith and confidence in their spirit guides and they were not disappointed. Here they are remembered with love and awe, and as the group experimental sittings with the scientists have now terminated at the request of the spirit guides, we are all beginning to realise how tremendously privileged we were to witness such divine happenings.

Mr. Monty Keen took this photograph immediately after a sitting by The Scole Experimental Group in April 1997. The wind chime and cowbells can be seen hanging from above. In the foreground is the small table on which Robin had his tape recorder and in the centre is the round table that was levitated and moved at each sitting. The crystals appeared to be undisturbed in spite of the antics of the table!

Note: The Scole mediums had wide and positive coverage in the world's Press and two excellent documentaries were created:

1. The Afterlife Investigations by Tim Coleman (DVD 86 minutes) and
2. The Afterlife Experiments (DVD 90 minutes) by Alliance Motion Pictures PTY Ltd.

Both are excellent documentaries on the Scole mediums and their pioneering work in psychic research.

37.

During my long career as a professional medium I was privileged to meet many celebrities and was able to demonstrate my spiritual gifts to them. None of this could have happened without those who had gone before me lighting the path and revealing what could be achieved. I have the deepest respect for the mediums that allowed me to witness their amazing gifts and encouraged me to follow with the development of my own psychic awareness. I know I have been able to help many thousands of people in the process and that has given me deep satisfaction.

Looking back on my somewhat adventurous life, my Indian travels and my continuous studies of this amazing subject I know I have not included all who participated in my development. I hope they will forgive me and accept that they are also loved and remembered fondly.

Here I should remember one tiny lady who graciously entertained me at her flat in Ladbroke Square London many years ago. She showed me a book filled with communications from deceased friends and family who had succeeded in writing messages in their exact earthly handwriting through an old-fashioned fountain pen she merely rested against her fingers. Being an orthodox Christian and churchgoer this phenomena had not been developed without a great deal of soul-searching. The lady was preparing for marriage to a pen-friend who lived in

Vancouver, Canada, when he had a sudden heart attack and died. The fiancé was Gordon Burdick, a naval man she had known for some years and she was devastated by his loss.

In her book "Beyond the Horizon" published in 1961, Grace Rosher explains some of her dilemma in reconciling her experience of spirit communication with her Christian faith. "I passed at times through quite agonizing periods of doubt, fearing lest I might be the victim of some strange hallucination, or of unconscious self-deception. I wanted desperately to believe, but dare I, that this wonderful thing was true?"

She sought help from the Rev. John D. Pearce-Higgins, Vice-chairman of The Churches' Fellowship for Psychical Study. Clergymen as well as friends witnessed messages being conveyed through the "magic" fountain pen that merely rested against Grace's outstretched finger. A moving film was taken of the pen in action. The pen moved forward on the paper producing words that claimed to be from various individuals who had made their transition to the spirit world, Gordon being the main communicator. The letter 't' was never crossed and the letter 'i' never dotted. Slowly the pen lifted itself off the paper at the end of each word, moved forward and wrote the next word in the message. Grace herself would intervene with regular questions to the spirit and would then wait for the answer. Her book has photographs of many handwriting samples received from the other world. Mr. Hilliger, a handwriting specialist was given samples of

Gordon's writing while on earth to compare with those received through the fountain pen. He declared them to be almost identical except for the missing crossbar on the 't' and the 'i' with no dot. The BBC showed the film on a late-night television programme about life beyond. In my opinion it should have been shown at prime-time when many more viewers could have witnessed the event.

Grace constantly tested Gordon in order to convince herself that he was not some kind of evil spirit impersonating her loved one. At one stage Gordon replied: "The fact that we have entered a new phase of life does not mean that we are able to behave like crooks more easily than before, also we are associating with our own kind – those on the same mental and spiritual plane and not on a lower one. No, Grace, you can rest assured that I am your communicator and your guardian."

She also made Gordon aware that many people on earth who had heard of these things thought it all seemed too nice over there. Gordon replied: "There are very unpleasant parts of this world where those unhappy folk who have been greedy, cruel and selfish go to because they have made their own kind of hell for themselves. It is true that we reap what we sow and have to pay the price of our wrongdoing…When we recognise that we have done wrong and want to express our sorrow, we are given every opportunity to make amends and use our opportunity for helping others."

Gordon gave Grace many examples of how he had been taken down into various lower levels of existence with a team of helpers whose task it was to bring light and knowledge to many who were living in a state of gloom and ignorance and in so doing to assist them in their spiritual progress. In other words he was a kind of spiritual missionary in his world.

In her second book "The Travellers' Return" Grace relates how she had asked Gordon whether he could trace her five-times great-grandmother, a lady named Jane Holt who had died on December 25th, 1752. Grace and her sister Freda, with whom she resided, were in possession of Jane's fan, snuff-box, letters and verses that had been handed down as family heirlooms. Jane had been attached to the Court of King George II, was extremely well educated and had been a tutor to two generations of the royal family. Gordon agreed to search for this ancestor in his world. It took three years before he was able to write that he had found and brought Jane Holt with him. As this lady had only used a quill pen when on earth, she had to become comfortable with using Grace's fountain pen. Jane revealed that she had known Sir Christopher Wren and his family and that her father's name had been Thomas Wiseman, a fact not known by Grace.

As I held the notebook that Miss Rosher gave me I was able to compare the handwriting of Jane Holt from one of her original letters with that produced through the automatic writing. They were identical.

Grace had asked: "Do all the generations meet and mingle?"

"Yes," Jane replied, "because there is no past or future as we regarded it on earth, only the eternal present."

So it would appear that the inhabitants of the spirit world are outside time in their new dimension. Time has little meaning for them which probably explains why certain predictions made from their side of life have not always manifested correctly by our standards. We must always use our common sense when evaluating such things.

I am so grateful to have met Grace Rosher on a couple of occasions and to have visited her home for tea and conversation. On my second visit I took an 8mm movie projector and was able to entertain Grace and Freda with a showing of my Indian travels. Both ladies were vegetarians. Grace's birthday was on 14th October (Libra) and she had been a nurse in the Red Cross during the Second World War. An oil painting hung on the wall in her front passageway showing her in nurse's uniform and she was certainly a well-educated lady and one who was not easily taken in by trickery. She seemed so matter-of-fact and down-to-earth that one would hardly associate such happenings with her. She passed into the spirit world in 1980, the year I came to the United States as a mature student.

Although I never witnessed the pen in action, Grace kindly allowed me access to the various notebooks that had been used by Gordon and several other communicators well-known in psychic research. In addition to her spiritual pursuits Grace was a talented portrait painter and some of her miniatures had been exhibited at The Royal Academy.

I took this photo of Grace Rosher in the gardens opposite her ground floor flat in Ladbroke Square, London W. 11. She was a very charming lady with a lively mind and a cultured background. Her amazing contribution to our understanding of what happens after we die has not been fully recognized. Gordon's accounts of his after-life experiences are well worth reading no matter what one's religious affiliations may be. To spread truth is what really matters.

EPILOGUE

If you have been inspired by my story and it has helped to improve your faith in a life to come and given you a sense of purpose then I can only have succeeded in my aim. Many people have wanted to learn how to do the work I do. I can only assure them it is not easy and there may be many 'growing pains' in the process. None of us is perfect. We are all here on earth to learn love, service and compassion, in the nature of Jesus, Buddha and all the great teachers. One occult principle is "Resist not evil, but overcome evil with good." It makes total sense that we concentrate our thoughts upon that which is positive and healing rather than the negative and the destructive. When, for example, we educate our children about the deceptive world of drugs and why they should avoid them, we are giving the children understanding that the world is a place of choice and that bad things can happen to the ignorant. Such education *is* necessary.

May each one of us be enlightened and guided by higher principles in making those choices and consequently be aware that as we *think*, so do we *attract*, and also *become*. One day we will make our transition to that incredible world of the universal mind matrix. There, all our thoughts and desires will be recognised, and many of them will be materialised as part of the reality in our astral environment. We should therefore watch our thoughts, avoid wasting our time on negative pursuits and endeavour to do a little good each day. When Jesus said, "In my

Father's house are many mansions" he was seeking to educate us about the need for good conduct in order that we may be received into a level of peace, harmony and love. Therefore do no harm, develop your individual talents to the best of your ability and remember that God's universal plan is infinite diversity not sickening conformity! Each of us has a different face, figure and personality with variable needs. What may be *right* for one may be totally *wrong* for another. It is not for us to judge. Through the DNA of our parents, God has given us all a different appearance and individuality for self-expression. May we long honour those differences, develop them, and in so doing, love and respect our neighbour.

At seventy-six years of age I was advised by my spirit friends that it was time for me to retire and begin to enjoy the rest of my life. In 2012 I bought an older home in Palm Springs at a very reasonable price, upgraded it with security gates and new tiled floors in the bedrooms. Where there had been only stones I planted flowers and slowly gathered a collection of plants that I could enjoy. I gave my last group demonstration in October 2013 and I know that I will be missed by so many lovely people who visited me over the years. I thank all of you for your kind support and input. I have learned much from all of you. After moving from Yarmouth Avenue Ramesh assisted me greatly by arranging for the rental of that former residence and he has now joined me in the desert. As he was from Ahmedabad in India he has in a sense returned to a desert community. As a teenager I read widely about Lawrence of Arabia and his "Seven Pillars of Wisdom" and felt some kind of connection with the desert and that period. Now I am enjoying my studio in Palm Springs with its peaceful environment that allows me to concentrate upon recording my experiences and putting them out for you, the reader, to share. I do hope you have enjoyed this book, imperfect as it may be.

Please remember that promotion of any published work is an expensive business. This autobiography has been considerably revised and brought out at a much lower cost than the original publication. If you have enjoyed this account of my life please recommend it to your friends and help spread the great truth of survival. Thank you and peace be with you!

BRIAN EDWARD HURST
Palm Springs, California U.S.A.
April, 2018.

Made in the USA
Las Vegas, NV
08 June 2022

49967727R00184